EXTRAORDINARY PEOPLE
of the
Harlem Renaissance

P. STEPHEN HARDY &
SHEILA JACKSON HARDY

EXTRAORDINARY PEOPLE
of the
Harlem Renaissance

Children's Press®
A Division of Grolier Publishing
New York   London   Hong Kong   Sydney
Danbury, Connecticut

To Vaughn Noelle Jackson who has loved Langston Hughes from the first poem of his I read to her and to Naziem Dalton Flanigan and all the children of the world who need to know.

Consultant: Alice Adamczyk, New York Public Library, Schomberg Collection

Visit Children's Press on the Internet at *http://publishing.grolier.com*

Book production by Editorial Directions, Inc.

Library of Congress Cataloging-in-Publication Data
Hardy, P. Stephen.
      Extraordinary people of the Harlem Renaissance / P. Stephen Hardy and Sheila Jackson Hardy.
      144 p. 24 cm. — (Extraordinary people)
      Includes bibliographical references and index.
      Summary : Looks at the many artists, photographers, choreographers, musicians, composers,
poets, writers, and other creative people who made Harlem such an amazing place in the 1920s and 1930s.
      ISBN 0-516-21201-X (lib. bdg.)   0-516-27170-9 (pbk.)
      1. Afro-American arts—New York (State)—New York—Biography—Juvenile literature. 2.
Arts, Modern—20th century—New York (State)—New York—Juvenile literature. 3. Harlem
Renaissance—Juvenile literature. [1. Harlem Renaissance. 2. Artists. 3. Afro-Americans—Biography. 4.
Afro-American arts. 5. Arts, Modern—20th century.] I. Hardy, Sheila Jackson. II. Title. III. Series.
NX512.3.A35 H37 2000
700'.92'39607307471—dc21
[B]   99-043629

Acknowledgments

We would like to thank Patricia C. McKissack and Frederick L. McKissack for touching our lives with their friendship, their example, and their encouragement.

Contents

115

Claude McKay
1890–1948
Writer and Poet

131

Nora Zeale Hurston
1901–1960
Writer and
Anthropologist

146

Carl Van Vechten
1880–1964
Writer and
Photographer

119

Jean Toomer
1894–1967
Writer and Poet

135

Wallace Thurman
1902–1934
Writer and Editor

152

**Patrons of the
Harlem Renaissance**

125

Arnaud "Arna" Bontemps
1902–1973
Writer and Educator

139

Jessie Redmon Fauset
1882–1961
Writer

161

Mary Edmonia Lewis
1845– ?
Sculptor

128

Nella Larsen
1891–1964
Writer

143

Sterling Allen Brown
1901–1989
Writer and Poet

168

Henry Ossawa Tanner
1859–1937
Painter

174

May Howard Jackson
1877–1931
Sculptor

192

James Van Der Zee
1886–1983
Photographer and
Photojournalist

213

Richmond Barthé
1901–1989
Sculptor

178

Meta Vaux Warrick Fuller
1877–1968
Sculptor

196

Laura Wheeler Waring
1887–1948
Painter

220

Hale Aspacio Woodruff
1900–1980
Painter and Educator

182

Nancy Elizabeth Prophet
1890–1960
Sculptor

200

William Henry Johnson
1901–1970
Painter

225

Palmer C. Hayden
1890–1973
Painter

186

Aaron Douglas
1899–1979
Painter

208

Archibald Motley Jr.
1891–1981
Painter

230

Horace Pippin
1888–1946
Painter

Preface

As we researched this era, we learned that some historians feel that the leaders of the Harlem Renaissance were foolish to believe that racism would end if African-Americans could show white people that they were not inferior by excelling in the arts and literature. Despite the success of many African-Americans, racism remained their biggest problem.

The Harlem Renaissance had many positive effects. For the first time, African-Americans had an opportunity to express themselves creatively for the entire world to see. They produced many "firsts": the first African-American to have a best-selling novel, the first African-American woman to graduate from Columbia University in New York, the first African-American romantic storyline performed onstage, the first big band orchestra, and more. These pioneering efforts opened the door for other African-Americans and influenced an entire generation of young artists and writers.

It was truly an amazing experience to read the personal thoughts of people such as Alain Locke, Marcus Garvey, Langston Hughes, W. E. B. Du Bois, Arna Bontemps, and Wallace Thurman. We could see our own contemporary challenges of being writer and artist were often very similar to the personal struggles of these Harlem Renaissance icons. During many periods of history, it has been difficult to document the black experience because our participation in many aspects of America's development and world history was kept hidden to perpetuate the myth of black inferiority. But the artists of the Harlem Renaissance ensured their contributions were well documented. Black newspapers, literary magazines, photographs, and the books themselves are a living testament to their contributions. Almost as extraordinary as the people was the joy of researching this topic in the new millennium. With the Internet, we were able to see and hear the Harlem Renaissance. We listened to the music of W. C. Handy, the voice of Bessie Smith, and a recording of Countee Cullen reading his poetry. We viewed the art of the Harlem Renaissance, in addition to the many photographs of Harlem life taken by James Van Der Zee, Morgan and Marvin Smith, and James Latimer Allen.

Being a writer, artist, or entertainer is an extremely difficult career path for African-Americans, even today. We cannot imagine what it must have felt like to be a creative person in the 1920s and 1930s, when discrimination was rampant and lynching black people was an acceptable practice. The individuals selected for this book are truly extraordinary because they succeeded at a time when African peoples were believed to be inferior.

Many writers, artists, and entertainers are associated with the Harlem Renaissance because their work was greatly influenced by that era, though the contributions of these individuals were not significant until the mid-1930s and later, after the era had ended. We made a special effort to include the biographies of those who played an important role in laying the groundwork for the New Negro movement and those whose contributions were at their height during the Harlem Renaissance years.

The extraordinary people of the Harlem Renaissance that we selected for this book are not included merely for their achievements. They are included because of the harsh circumstances under which they triumphed. To be extraordinary during the 1920s required far more than raw talent. It required great courage and dedication—qualities that we can all admire.

The New Negro

A positive self-image—there was cause for one—was considered the best starting point for a better chance. Inequities due to race might best be removed when reasonable men saw that black men were thinkers, strivers, doers, and were cultured, like themselves. . . . And such achievement, because it was elite in character, was a source of race pride and an argument against continued discrimination.

—Nathan Irvin Huggins, historian

The Harlem Renaissance began only fifty-six years after slavery had ended. African-Americans were moving north in great numbers. The South remained a difficult and dangerous place for African-Americans to live. Jim Crow laws, white-on-black violence, and lack of work made it very hard for black people to survive. When World War I began, it created thousands of jobs for black Americans. The North was the industrial sector of the United States, where high wages were paid to factory workers and miners. In addition, more than 350,000 African-Americans served in the armed forces.

For African-Americans, the North was a safe haven as well as a land of opportunity. It has been estimated that between 1920 and 1925, more than

The 369th Infantry Division, World War I

2 million black people moved from the South to the North. There was a strong feeling of progress and the hope that life in the North would be sweeter. Finally African-Americans would have the opportunity to break away from the limitations of small-town life—to do what they wanted to do and be who they wanted to be. These ideas and hopes gave birth to the New Negro. But even in the North, there were obstacles to overcome. The first obstacle to face was a poor self-image.

Today, we understand culture to mean all the ideas, customs, skills, and arts that make a group of people unique. But at the turn of the century in

America, culture could be achieved only by leaving behind one's ethnic identity. One had to learn the behaviors that were considered "proper" and acceptable to upper-class whites. American schools taught that culture was not the way your parents talked and behaved. Culture did not have accents, or dialects, or "old folks' tales." The question remained, some fifty-six years after slavery, whether black Americans had achieved a level of culture that would make them equal in the eyes of white Americans.

The second obstacle was white America's belief that African-Americans were, by nature, inferior. The leaders of the Harlem Renaissance believed that once it was proven that blacks were, indeed, the equal of whites, the walls of prejudice would come crumbling down. Truth would be their weapon against the lies that fueled racial discrimination. Black nationalist Marcus Garvey was one of the first to proclaim that Africa was the birthplace of human civilization, fine art, science, and culture.

The New Negro would not quietly ask for his fair share of the fruits of democracy. During World War I, the 369th Infantry Regiment had proven that the Negro was willing to fight for freedom and justice in Europe and at home. In the summer of 1919, "the Red Summer," white Americans rioted in more than twenty cities, killing blacks and destroying their property. In the face of such violence, the New Negro demanded that America live up to its promise of liberty and justice for all.

The art and literature of the Harlem Renaissance focused on proving the humanity and equality of African-Americans. Meta Vaux Warrick Fuller's sculpture *Ethiopia Awakening* symbolized the spirit of the early stages of the Renaissance. It portrayed African peoples as awakening from the dark days of oppression to the dawn of a new day of achievements. Claude McKay's poem "If We Must Die" spoke forcefully against the racial violence that gripped the United States. Entertainers such as Paul Robeson refused roles that were demeaning to African-Americans. Activists W. E. B. Du Bois and

A Harlem street scene, 1920s

James Weldon Johnson criticized the failure of America to protect all citizens and asserted the value of black American life and history.

The Harlem Renaissance opened the doors of opportunity to black Americans in roles that had once been considered unreachable—university professors, best-selling authors, diplomats, internationally acclaimed celebrities, and more. Despite these successes, the New Negro fell short of his most cherished goal—equality.

As early as 1903, W. E. B. Du Bois called on white America to take responsibility for its part in the race problem. Although progress had been made, it had been essentially left to African-Americans to do the work of solving the race issue. When the 1929 stock-market crash brought on the Great Depression, America's focus and funding were taken away from the issues of prejudice and inequality. Without the participation of white America, the Renaissance was halted before it reached its final goal. But the spirit of the New Negro lived on.

New generations of African-Americans such as Romare Bearden, Ralph Ellison, Toni Morrison, Richard Wright, Dr. Martin Luther King Jr., Angela Davis, and the Reverend Jesse Jackson have continued to work for peace and equality—keeping the Renaissance spirit alive.

God and Nature first made us what we are, and then out of our own creative genius we make ourselves what we want to be. Follow always that great law. Let the sky and God be our limit, and Eternity our measurement. There is no height to which we cannot climb by using the active intelligence of our own minds.

—Marcus Garvey

William Edward Burghardt (W. E. B.) Du Bois

Sociologist, Educator, and Political Activist
1868–1963

*O*ne ever feels his twoness —An American, a Negro; two souls, two thoughts, two unreconciled strivings . . . in one dark body. . . . He simply wishes to make it possible for a man to be both a Negro and an American, without being cursed and spit upon by his fellows, without having the doors of Opportunity closed roughly in his face.

William Edward Burghardt (W. E. B.) Du Bois was born in Great Barrington, Massachusetts, February 23, 1868. He was a child of mixed race whose father walked away from the family. His mother, a determined woman, raised him by herself.

Very little prejudice existed in Great Barrington. William played and went to school with his white neighbors. An incident with a girl who had just moved to Great Barrington, however, made him aware that he was different from his friends. He had the sudden feeling that he was "shut out from their world by a vast veil." William became determined that he would not be kept from having the same opportunities and rewards available to those in the white world beyond the veil.

William excelled in school, and the community of Great Barrington raised money for him to attend a university. William fully expected to be sent to nearby Harvard or Amherst College. Instead, the town sent him to Fisk University, an all-black school in the South.

While at Fisk, Du Bois found himself surrounded by black men whose experiences with racism and poverty were far beyond anything that he had known. Du Bois and his mother were poor, but it was nothing compared to the spirit-breaking poverty of the rural South. He decided then that he must do everything he could to exterminate racism and its effects on African-Americans.

Du Bois's class work was excellent. He graduated in 1888 and made his way, at last, to Harvard University. Du Bois had changed, though, and Harvard was not as grand and appealing to him as it had been before his experience in the South.

At Harvard, Du Bois earned a master's degree, a doctorate, and a fellowship to study for two years at the University of Berlin in Germany. He returned to America with an unshakable belief that scientific research could expose racial injustices. He was sure that once the truth was exposed, white people would be moved to do their part to make things right.

To accomplish this, Du Bois pioneered the scientific study of racial conflict. A shocking revelation, however, convinced him that science alone would not be enough to turn the violent tide of racism. He was walking to a meeting with the editor of the *Atlanta Constitution,* a black newspaper, when he saw on display in a grocery-store window the mangled knuckles of an African-American who had recently been lynched. Du Bois knew he could no longer be a cool, detached scientist while his brethren were being brutally killed without hope of protection from police or government. He came to believe that it would take aggressive protest and political action to end the evils of racism. These ideas were directly opposed to those of Booker T. Washington, the most widely known and respected African-American leader at that time.

Booker T. Washington believed that African-Americans needed self-esteem and pride in themselves to advance in white-dominated society. He called on blacks to work together to build businesses, agriculture, and wealth, which he felt would give them power and the respect of whites. Du Bois agreed with those ideas but felt many of Washington's other ideas and programs were holding back the progress of African-Americans.

Washington did not believe in higher education as a means of "uplifting the race." He stated that blacks themselves were responsible for their lowly position in America. His plan called for blacks to accept discrimination for now and be patient as they worked to better their lives and earn white respect. Southern and northern whites alike applauded that message.

Many blacks were afraid to stand up and demand equal treatment as Americans. They'd had enough of violence and hoped that Washington's plan would help to stop the killing of black people and the burning of black towns.

Many other African-Americans, however, felt Washington's approach was wrong and could only lead to more years of oppression. It was no easy task, though, to disagree with Booker T. Washington. He was a powerful man with strong supporters, both white and black, ready to squash those who spoke out against his policies. Du Bois, with the release of his book, *The Souls of Black Folk* in 1903, became the main spokesman for those opposed to Booker T. Washington.

In his book, Du Bois presented a clear, logical, and scientific explanation of the causes and effects of the race problem in America. He also, firmly but respectfully, pointed out the flaws in Washington's plan for black uplift. Du Bois showed where African-Americans were failing to do their part to take advantage of opportunities to better their situation. But he did not stop there.

He strongly stated that whites had to take their share of the responsibility for the racial problems of America. They could not continue to lay all the blame on the black man and woman. No one before Du Bois had so clearly and completely analyzed the race issue and presented it for all to see.

In July 1905, Du Bois organized a meeting in Niagara Falls, Ontario, Canada, for those African-Americans who wanted to challenge the ideas and leadership of Booker T. Washington. That group became known as the Niagara Movement. In February 1909, a group of white people who were also outraged by America's treatment of its black citizens joined the movement. Together, they formed the National Association for the Advancement of Colored People (NAACP).

Du Bois became the association's director of research and was editor of its monthly magazine, the *Crisis,* from 1910 until 1934. The *Crisis* inspired blacks nationwide and brought to them the ideas and plans of "Negro militant protest" to end racial injustice. It also featured the poetry and art of the Harlem Renaissance.

With the *Crisis,* Du Bois showed not only the injustice of America but also the beauty and achievements of African-Americans. Because painting,

The Crisis *office*

sculpture, literature, and music were believed to be the proof of cultural achievement, Du Bois encouraged blacks to excel in those areas, as well as in education. The pages of the *Crisis* were filled with black pride, black beauty, and examples of black achievement.

Du Bois fought many political battles to win equal rights for African-Americans. Together with James Weldon Johnson, he tried to get the U.S. government to stop lynching. But neither presidents nor Congress would stop whites from lynching blacks, or punish the ones who did.

As the leader of the Pan-African movement, Du Bois took the problems of African-Americans to an international level. He organized the Pan-African Congresses of 1900, 1919, 1921, and 1923. These conferences brought together leaders from Africa, America, and the Caribbean and addressed common issues facing people of African descent. Du Bois wanted whites and blacks all over the world to understand the full scope of racism so that men and women of goodwill would stand up and fight against it.

Du Bois firmly believed that education could end discrimination. He felt that the educated black elite, the "talented tenth" as he called them, could lead America to equality for its entire people. He used science and logic, politics and economics, art and literature to move the nation toward its stated position of freedom and justice for all. But America was not ready to live up to those ideals.

At the age of ninety-five, Du Bois gave up on America. He moved to Ghana in West Africa in 1961, renounced his U.S. citizenship, and became a Ghanaian citizen. He died on August 27, 1963, in Accra, Ghana.

Du Bois wrote that blacks "may and must criticize America, describe how she has ruined her democracy . . . and led her seats of justice astray." His open criticism and inspiring leadership were a bright beacon of hope and pride to African-Americans during the Harlem Renaissance and for many years after. His support and publicizing of the work of the artists and writers of the Renaissance helped to awaken America to the wonderful contributions of its black citizens.

Marcus Garvey

Activist and Publisher
1887–1940

I was not made to be whipped. It annoys me to be defeated; hence to me, to be once defeated is to find cause for an everlasting struggle to reach the top.

These are the determined words of Marcus Mosiah Garvey, by far the most controversial political figure of the Harlem Renaissance. He organized the largest international black movement in history and his influence was felt worldwide.

Born in St. Ann's Bay, Jamaica, in 1887, Marcus was

the youngest of eleven children. He turned out to be a lot like his father, whom he described as "severe, firm, determined, bold, and strong, refusing to yield even to superior forces if he believed he was right."

In the late 1800s in Jamaica, skin color, social value, and economic status were directly related, with the white community being the most wealthy, while the mulattoes achieved middle-class, and the "unmixed Negroes" were the poor underclass. Marcus was born into poverty.

At the age of fourteen, Marcus was sent to Kingston, Jamaica, to apprentice with his godfather for three years to learn the trade of printing. Though he resented being removed from school, he excelled as a master printer and foreman. An incident with the printer's union first prompted Marcus to become an activist. He was the only foreman to take part in a strike. When the striking workers were given back their jobs, Garvey was not reinstated. Garvey became interested in politics and traveled from 1910 to 1911 to see what life was like for black people in other countries.

> I started to take an interest in the politics of my country, and then I saw
> the injustice done to my race because it was black. . . . I went traveling to
> South and Central America and parts of the West Indies to find out if it
> was so elsewhere, and I found the same situation. I set sail for Europe and
> again I found the same stumbling block—"You are black."

While in Costa Rica and Panama, Garvey put his printing talent to work and published two newspapers, *La Nacionale* and *La Prensa*. He used his newspapers to expose the plight of migrant workers who were being abused and exploited. In 1912, Marcus went to England. There he resumed his education and attended law classes at Birkbeck College in London. He met and befriended people from Africa and learned of their similar struggles for independence and justice. The more Garvey heard, the more he began to

A UNIA parade

think about ways to help the people of Africa and the Africans who settled in other countries. Eager to put his ideas into action, he returned to Jamaica in 1914 and began the United Negro Improvement Association (the UNIA) and African Communities League. The international group's mission was to unite all African people of the world. Another focus of the UNIA was to enable African people to take an active role in educating themselves. Garvey admired Booker T. Washington, the founder of Tuskegee University. He wrote Washington and told him of his desire to visit him in the United States because he wanted to learn how to set up his own university. In 1915, Booker T. Washington died. But by 1916, Garvey came to the United States and opened the first U.S. chapter of the UNIA in Harlem, New York.

Garvey had learned public speaking by imitating ministers who preached in the streets. He started out preaching his African nationalist views from a soapbox on Lenox Avenue. Then he published his views in his own newspaper, the *Negro World*. From 1918 to 1933, worldwide circulation reached as high as 200,000, making the *Negro World* the most widely read black paper of its era.

The Black Star Line Steamship Corporation was Garvey's greatest ambition, and his greatest disappointment. In 1919, he began the line of ships, which included the SS *Yarmouth* (renamed the SS *Frederick Douglass*), the SS *Shadyside*, and the SS *Kanawha*. Many misunderstood Garvey's intentions and believed the ships were intended to transport African people back to Africa. Garvey's belief was that African people needed to reclaim their homeland by helping rid Africa of white colonists who had taken over many African countries and abused the people. By restoring Africa to its greatness, black people around the world would have a power base—a government of their own from which they could draw. His plan for the ships was to establish trade and commerce between Africans in America, the Caribbean, South and Central America, Canada, and Africa. He sold shares in his venture for $5 each. At the same time he launched several successful businesses. Through his Negroes Factories Association (NFA), he opened a chain of cooperative grocery stores, a restaurant, a milliner, a steam laundry, a tailor and dressmaking shop, and a publishing house.

By 1920, when the Harlem Renaissance was underway, Garvey had organized the UNIA's first convention. There were 2,000 delegates in attendance from UNIA chapters around the globe, and a total of 25,000 people packed New York's Madison Square Garden. At the convention, delegates decided on the organization's official colors—"red for the blood shed in black struggle; black as a symbol of pride; and green for the new life in Africa." The convention opened and closed with a huge parade, the hallmark of UNIA festivities. The participants were ordinary people dressed like soldiers, nurses, and airmen. His rifle corps wore colorful uniforms designed in military style. The Black Cross nurses dressed in white and marched more than 200 strong along with the UNIA band, the choir, the Universal Africa Motor Corps, the Black Eagle Flying Corps, and the juvenile auxiliary.

After the convention, Garvey was the most popular man in Harlem. His emphasis on education and his belief that black people should take pride in their African history and culture made him a powerful voice for the New Negro movement. His words inspired thousands to buy shares in the Black Star Line. The UNIA supported military training, nursing, and engineering classes, along with education in African and African-American history. Garvey's efforts to uplift the race drew the attention of the Bureau of Investigation (later renamed the Federal Bureau of Investigation [FBI]), who began to watch Marcus closely.

According to the UNIA records, its U.S. membership ultimately exceeded 1 million, in addition to 120,000 members in the Caribbean and Latin America, and another 30,000 in Africa. The UNIA's second convention, in 1921, was even more successful than the first. In 1922, because of an illegal act performed by one of the officers of the Black Star Line, Garvey and three other company officials were charged with mail fraud. Garvey believed that the charges were the result of a setup. Feeling he could not trust anyone and unwilling to use a white attorney, he presented his own case in court and lost. Garvey's new wife, Amy St. Jacques, made sure that the UNIA kept going despite the trial and her husband's absence. In 1922, the third annual UNIA convention went on as planned, with increasing membership support of their leader.

Garvey appealed the court's decision but his appeal was denied. Even many of his critics viewed this as unjust. W. E. B. Du Bois of the NAACP spoke out on behalf of the controversial leader. The *New York Evening Bulletin* wrote, "Garvey is a Negro, but even a Negro is entitled to have the truth told about him." Garvey was sentenced to five years in jail and a $1,000 fine. While in prison, he wrote about his life and his beliefs. Amy edited his essays and published a volume of his writings and speeches in 1923, and another collection of essays, *Philosophy and Opinions of Marcus Garvey,* in 1925. There was a fifth UNIA conference in 1926, in which the organization stepped up its efforts to free Garvey. By December 1927, Garvey was released, but the government ordered his immediate return to Jamaica.

Garvey continued his political activism and the work of the UNIA until his death in London in 1940. His influence can be seen in the marches of the civil rights movement of the 1960s and the Black Power movement of the 1970s. His philosophy contributed to the development of the Nation of Islam and the Rastafarian religion.

Garvey's biography begins with the words of his wife. In her tribute, she explains that when a leader comes forth with ideas and historical information that has not yet been proved or widely accepted, he is likely to be called crazy, dangerous, or foolish. She continues, "Long after the leader's death, when the truths . . . or dangers which he pointed out came to pass, then they . . . are prone to admit that the visionary was right, and must have been inspired to be so persevering." That visionary was Marcus Garvey.

Alain Leroy Locke

Educator and Arts Advocate
1886–1954

Of all the voluminous literature on the Negro, so much is mere external view and commentary . . . that nine-tenths of it is about the Negro rather than of him, so that it is the Negro problem rather than the Negro that is known. . . . Whoever wishes to see the Negro . . . in the full perspective of his achievements and possibilities, must seek the enlightenment of that self portraiture which the present developments of Negro culture are offering.

On October 13, 1886, in Philadelphia, Pennsylvania,

Alain Leroy Locke was born to S. Pliny and Mary Hawkins Locke. His parents were unusually well educated for their time, and both were teachers.

Alain's father died when the boy was just six years old, and his mother raised him alone. She was determined that he receive the best education, and he did. Alain earned a scholarship to Harvard University and, in 1907, graduated magna cum laude. That same year he became the first African-American to win a Rhodes scholarship, allowing him to continue studying in Oxford, England.

The subject that attracted Locke's keen mind at Oxford was philosophy —the study of why people and cultures act the way they do. At Oxford, he also developed friendships with a number of well-educated Africans. Through them he gained a new perspective on America's racial problems and learned a great deal about Africa and its history.

Locke founded the African Union Society, with the goal of encouraging a sense of brotherhood and higher learning among its members, as future "leaders of the African Race." Members often discussed how the myth that Negroes and Asians were inferior to whites was linked to the Europeans' need to control their nonwhite colonies. It was quite a learning experience for one who had known only of racial conditions in the United States.

In addition, Locke discovered that the leading artists of Europe had been amazed by African tribal art and were using its classic forms to shake up their European art traditions. Locke returned to the United States with dreams of the glory that African-American artists would achieve, if only they could develop a connection to the arts of their ancestors.

In 1912, Locke began teaching English at Howard University in Washington, D.C. He wrote his first book, *Race Contacts and Inter-racial Relations,* in 1916. He remained fascinated with Africa and, in 1924, went to Egypt for the opening of the tomb of King Tutankhamen.

Locke wrote that the world's first truly great "cultural renaissance" took place in Africa. The Great Pyramids, science and mathematics, sculpture, and much else were all born of African civilizations. Locke realized few white scholars were willing to admit these facts.

Middle-class African-Americans, though, were not proud of their African ancestry. This was probably a result of the widespread theory that Africans were ignorant savages and had done nothing in all their history to advance human civilization. Though there was much evidence against this false idea, it was not well known at that time. Black Americans who wanted to improve their social and financial position in the United States often felt that the way to do so was to be as much "American" and as little "Negro" as possible. Poet Langston Hughes called this "the racial mountain." It kept blacks from being proud of their history and themselves. Hughes wrote:

> They go to white theatres and white movies . . . [adopt] Nordic [white] manners, Nordic faces, Nordic hair, [and] Nordic art (if any). . . . A very high mountain indeed for the . . . racial [black] artist to climb in order to discover himself and his people.

This way of thinking encouraged many African-Americans to try to be something they were not—white. Locke was determined to do something about this attitude.

In 1925, he edited a special issue of the mainstream cultural magazine, *Survey Graphic.* That issue, "Harlem: Mecca of the New Negro," sold out two printings. The success of the *Survey Graphic* issue led Locke to publish an extended version of it in a book titled *The New Negro: An Interpretation.* It has been called the most important book of the Harlem Renaissance.

The New Negro included historical and social essays, poetry, fiction, plays, critiques, and photographs of African sculpture—a diverse collection of subjects and art forms that stimulated thought and challenged the ideas of prejudice. It also included the artwork of Aaron Douglas. His exciting new way of portraying African peoples was, for thousands of Americans, the first evidence they'd seen that black artists existed in the United States.

The success of *The New Negro* led to Locke's becoming a consultant to Mary Beattie Brady, the director of the Harmon Foundation. The Harmon art exhibitions were the most important way for African-American artists to gain recognition for their work and careers. Through the Harmon exhibitions, black artists could achieve national recognition and the sales necessary to support themselves.

In his essays, critiques, and advice, Locke encouraged black American artists to do with their art what African artists had accomplished in the "ancestral arts"—to powerfully express their own lives, thoughts, and culture. He discouraged what he felt was simply imitating the works and culture of Europeans.

Locke also took talented African-Americans to wealthy patrons such as Charlotte Mason. These patrons gave artists the financial support they needed to quit their day jobs and spend more time perfecting their talents.

Locke continued to write on the importance of art in combating the racial stereotypes that worked to prevent a positive African-American self-image. Some artists were confused by his call to look to the "ancestral arts" for inspiration. They didn't see how copying African art forms could be meaningful to modern African-Americans. Others, including Aaron Douglas, Sargent Claude Johnson, and Richmond Barthé, did understand. They created impressive works combining black culture, identity, and history.

Like W. E. B. Du Bois, Locke wanted African-Americans to see beauty in themselves. His writings and promotion of African and African-American art were aimed at changing how black Americans saw themselves. Rather than copying white ways, he called on African-Americans to be proud of their blackness. Only then, he reasoned, would the race wake up and lead the world as it had in its historic days of glory.

Because of Locke's efforts, many black colleges added art instruction to their list of courses. Locke also promoted the teaching of what is now known as black studies. These courses increase the knowledge of the historic contributions of black civilizations all over the world, from ancient times to the present.

Locke played a crucial role in defining the New Negro movement and advancing the cause of African-American art and artists in the studio, the gallery, and in black colleges and universities. He retired from Howard University in 1953 and died of heart disease in New York in 1954. His studies of racial problems and his numerous essays and books on the cultural gifts of black Americans are still used as the basis for further study today. More than any other person, Alain Locke explained and defined the New Negro and the Harlem Renaissance.

James Weldon Johnson

Diplomat, Songwriter, Attorney, Journalist, Novelist, and Educator
1871–1938

The most outstanding phase of development of the New Negro during the past decade has been the recent literary and artistic emergence of the individual creative artist.

James Weldon Johnson was born in Jacksonville, Florida, in 1871. Though he was born in the South, his father had been a "free black" from Virginia who worked as a headwaiter at a local resort hotel. His mother, Helen, was a schoolteacher from the Bahamas.

Before the Harlem Renaissance had even begun, James had accomplished more than the average person does in a lifetime. In Jacksonville, African-Americans were not allowed to attend high schools, so Johnson left home to attend Atlanta University, which at that time was both a secondary school and a college. He spent his summers teaching in a poor black school in rural Georgia. Johnson was dedicated to fighting racism and improving the lives of African-Americans. By 1894, he was principal of a small school that he expanded into a high school for black children. The following year he founded the *Daily American,* the first newspaper in the United States directed toward African-Americans. Johnson completed a master's degree in music at Atlanta University and studied law as well. In 1897, he was the first African-American lawyer to be admitted to the Florida Bar Association. Three years later, he wrote a poem that he and his brother Rosamond put to music. That song, "Lift Every Voice and Sing," is now celebrated as the Negro national anthem. In 1901, Johnson moved to New York to pursue his love for music. He and Rosamond, with composer Bob Cole, wrote more than 200 songs for musical theater.

During this period, Johnson enrolled in creative-writing classes at Columbia University. He also became treasurer of the Colored Republicans Club, supporting the ideas of activist Booker T. Washington. In turn, Washington put in a good word on Johnson's behalf, and President Theodore Roosevelt appointed him to the post of U.S. consul in Puerto Cabello, Venezuela, in 1906. His new position did not require a great deal of work, which left him free to write. His poems were published in the *Century* and the *Independent.* Johnson remained in Venezuela for three years until he was promoted to a new and more demanding position in Nicaragua in 1912. It was a time of intense political unrest in that Central American country, and Johnson was called to assist the U.S. government in placing military troops in Nicaragua.

That same year, Johnson published the novel *The Autobiography of an Ex-Colored Man* anonymously. This tragic tale was the story of a mulatto man who could not overcome the racial barriers that prevented him from having the music career he desired. After seeing a black man lynched, the main character loses hope and decides to pass for white.

In 1913, Johnson left the foreign service. He considered going home to Florida. But he knew that he could not return to the harsh racial climate there. So, in 1914, he returned to New York, and in 1916, took a job as an editorial writer for the oldest African-American newspaper in the city, the *New York Age*. New York was beginning to change already in the years before the Harlem Renaissance. It seemed the place to be was uptown, closer to Harlem. His brother Rosamond Johnson was the first African-American to purchase a home west of Lenox Avenue, on West 136th Street. James and his wife soon moved to an apartment near James's brother at 185 West 135th Street.

Johnson's editorials reflected his tireless dedication to the advancement of black people. W. E. B. Du Bois saw an opportunity to add Johnson as a top executive of the National Association for the Advancement of Colored People (NAACP) and urged Joel Spingarn, the organization's chairman, to hire Johnson. In 1917, he became the first African-American to serve as executive secretary of the NAACP and traveled all over the country opening new chapters of the organization. He became a political activist, fighting for anti-lynching legislation and bringing about the signing of the Dyer Anti-Lynching Bill of 1921. Along with Du Bois, Alain Locke, and Marcus Garvey, Johnson emerged as one of the leaders of the New Negro movement. He approached injustice with a three-step plan— legal action, political pressure, and publicity. His method was so effective it is still used by civil rights activists.

In 1920, Johnson visited Haiti to investigate the impact of the U.S.

military presence there. He returned disturbed by the abuses he saw. That same year he wrote several articles in the *Nation* magazine about his experience and published a book of poetry called *Self-Determining Haiti.* James Weldon Johnson made several important contributions to the literature of the Harlem Renaissance. In 1922, he edited *The Book of American Negro Poetry.* Along with his brother Rosamond and composer Bob Cole, Johnson was committed to preserving spirituals. So they collected and created musical scores for these songs, many of which had never been put on paper. Between 1925 and 1926, James and his brother published their collection of Negro spirituals. His 1912 novel, *The Autobiography of an Ex-Colored Man,* was published again in 1927, this time under his own name. The subject of light-skinned blacks passing as white was upsetting and fascinating at the same time and attracted readers of both races.

Johnson's early work in rural Georgia inspired his most celebrated book, *God's Trombones: Seven Negro Sermons in Verse* (1927). Written in the language of the rural South, he wanted to show "the genuine folk stuff that clings around the old time Negro preacher." Like his book of spirituals, this was another symbol of his commitment to celebrate the original folk culture of African-Americans. Johnson had convinced the Julius Rosenwald Fund to provide fellowships for African-American artists and writers. His next book, *Black Manhattan,* was funded by one of these fellowships. *Black Manhattan* examined the history of black people in that city and expressed hope for the future of the New Negro.

In 1931, Johnson was appointed to the Adam J. Spence Chair of Creative Literature at Fisk University. Maintaining a career as a writer, along with his duties with the NAACP, had become too exhausting, so Johnson accepted the appointment. For the first time, he was able to concentrate on writing and teaching. He soon published his autobiography, *Along This Way* (1933), and *Negro Americans, What Now?* (1934).

In 1938, Johnson died when a train struck the car he was in. At the 1939 world's fair, artist Augusta Savage honored his contribution with a sculpture titled *Lift Every Voice and Sing.* Shortly afterward, his friend writer Carl Van Vechten established the James Weldon Johnson Memorial Collection of Negro Arts and Letters at Yale University.

The Jazz Age

"More Jasbo. More Jas. More," the audience yelled. It is said that the term *jazz* was a variation of the name of Chicago musician Jasbo Brown. But the music of jazz existed before the name did, and it began much farther south. Like spirituals and blues, jazz had its roots in the South. The development of jazz can be traced along the banks of the Mississippi River from the small towns of Mississippi to cities such as Memphis, New Orleans, St. Louis, Kansas City, and then Chicago. About the same time that the Harlem Renaissance began, musicians such as Fletcher Henderson had begun to make their way to New York, playing a brand-new sound that was uniquely African-American.

When jazz arrived in New York, the Harlem elite had no interest in supporting a new black music form. The early Harlem Renaissance was designed to prove that African-Americans could be just as "cultured" as white Americans and excel in the arts and literature. Many feared that the new music would be unacceptable and looked down upon by white Americans.

Harlem Renaissance journalist and author Joel A. Rogers wrote, "The true spirit of jazz is a joyous revolt from convention, custom, authority, boredom, even sorrow—from everything that would confine the soul of man and hinder its riding free on air." Even the supposedly disapproving Harlem elite could not deny the infectious jazz rhythms. Piano player Willie "the Lion" Smith noted that "after a sedate parlor gathering and after the cabarets closed, poets and writers (even the occasional NAACP official) often would follow musicians to one of the nightly rent-paying rites." Harlem rent parties rocked with the loud blare of jazz, with piano professors such as James P. Johnson and Fats Waller tickling the ivories with their stride and boogie-woogie jazz styles. Admission usually cost a quarter.

It was the opening of the 1921 musical *Shuffle Along* that marked the beginning of the Jazz Age. It popularized the all-black revue and opened the door for more shows, including *Runnin' Wild, Blackbirds,* and *Hot Chocolates.* The city's nightlife had officially moved uptown. White New Yorkers were eager to experience the exotic African culture. During the Harlem Renaissance, it was fashionable for them to travel to Harlem to hear the Fletcher Henderson Rainbow Orchestra or the rhythmic scat singing of Louis Armstrong.

Arthur "Happy" Rhone was a pioneer of the American nightclub. His club Happy Rhone's was the first African-American nightspot to have a floor show. Then there was 133rd Street, also known as the Jungle. The Catagonia Club, The Bucket of Blood, Leroy's, Bank's, and Basement Brownies were on this street. The new Cotton Club and Connie's Inn were for "whites only." Singer Paul Robeson's favorite hideaway was Hayne's Oriental. And the best-kept secret of all was the Lybia.

If you could take the sound of jazz and turn it into movement, it would look like the Charleston. When we think of jazz today, we often imagine

The sheet music for "I'm Just Wild about Harry"

The Cotton Club

an easy, mellow sound, like the smooth notes of a saxophone. But the jazz of the 1920s was fast, wild, and free—and the dances that accompanied the music were no different. A *New York Herald* reporter described the athletic jazz dancers of *Shuffle Along* saying, "They fling their limbs about without stopping to make sure that they are securely fastened on."

Langston Hughes was among the first to embrace jazz music. His poetry flowed with the patterns and beats of this new African-American music, creating what is now referred to as jazz poetry. "I try to grasp and hold some of the meanings and rhythms of jazz," he said. "Jazz to me is one of the inherent expressions of Negro life in America: the eternal tom-tom beating in the Negro soul—the tom-tom of revolt against weariness in a white world, a world of subway trains, and work, work, work; the tom-tom of joy and laughter, and pain swallowed in a smile."

The art of the Harlem Renaissance also reflected the Jazz Age. Aaron Douglas believed the jazz musician symbolized freedom. His murals often featured the soulful image of a saxophone player. The paintings of Archibald Motley Jr. showed the world what it felt like to sit in a Harlem or Paris nightclub listening to jazz.

Harlem was in vogue and jazz meant style—from the tuxedo-clad orchestras of Duke Ellington to the colorful flair of King Oliver's Creole Jazz Band. Even rent parties moved Harlemites to don formal attire. The photography of James Van Der Zee showed Harlemites at their best. His 1932 "Portrait of a Couple with Raccoon Coats and Stylish Car" fully captured the proud sense of style that was Harlem.

Jazz rang in the spirit of the New Negro. It is still considered the most genuine expression of African-American life ever created—the black man's gift to the world.

Harry Herbert Pace and Black Swan Records

arry Herbert Pace was born in 1884 in Covington, Georgia, to Charles and Frances Pace. He was a brilliant student. By the age of nineteen, he was valedictorian of his graduating class at Atlanta University. During his studies at the university, he was a student of W. E. B. Du Bois, whom he admired and respected. This was several years before the start of the Harlem Renaissance. So when the national dialogue of the New Negro movement began in the 1920s, Harry was eager to do what he could to help further the cause of his former mentor.

In the early 1900s, virtually no black singers recorded with the major record labels and there were no black-owned record companies. The big record companies would routinely buy songs for their white singers from black songwriters and sheet music companies. Harry Herbert Pace and W. C. Handy were partners in one such company—Pace and Handy Sheet Music.

Pace had met W. C. Handy when he moved to Memphis in 1912. They became friends immediately and decided to work together writing songs and later formed their own sheet-music business in New York.

PARAMOUNT AND BLACK SWAN NOW ONE.

HARRY H. PACE

One of the most important episodes in the history of the phonograph record industry was the recent combination of The New York Recording Laboratories (recorders and manufacturers of Paramount records) and the Black Swan Phonograph Company repertoire.

By this merger, The New York Recording Laboratories has taken over all master records, contracts with talent and the good will of the Black Swan Company. Hereafter Black Swan records will be made under a special Paramount label.

This combination marks the unusual event of a merger of a large Negro company and a large white organization. It brings together the two leaders in the Race record field and now makes Paramount, more than ever, the unquestioned leader in the Race record business.

In a recent article published in the New York Age, President Harry H. Pace of the Black Swan Phonograph Company said:

"The Black Swan catalogue of several hundred master records is the most valuable of its kind in existence. Instead of the company operating that catalogue, the Paramount Company will manufacture and distribute Black Swan Records, from which the Black Swan Co. will receive a definite amount each month. After the Black Swan Co. has paid its own accounts and obligations, such as every operating company must have, it will be in a position to pay its stockholders a substantial and continuous dividend, or it can retire its capital stock at a substantial premium."

By Black Swan's combination with the Paramount Company—a white organization devoted to the interests of the Race and specializing in Race records—the continuance of high class Race music is assured.

* * * * * * * *

Lovie Austin just had a new picture taken, and we got it just in time to get it on the back page of this catalog. Lovie is the accomplished pianist who accompanies many of the Paramount stars when they sing Blues. She is the first girl of the Race to play the piano for records. Her famous Blues Serenaders have made themselves famous by their syncopating accompaniments, featuring Lovie at the piano and Tommy Ladinier with his mournful, praying cornet.

LOVIE AUSTIN

A magazine article on Pace and Black Swan Records

49

As the Harlem Renaissance gained momentum, there was a call for African-Americans to take control of their destinies and fight discrimination by starting businesses of their own that would employ and empower black people. Pace was tired of selling his songs to companies who refused to record blacks. So, in the spirit of the New Negro movement, he decided to end his partnership with W. C. Handy and formed the Pace Phonograph Corporation, and his own record label—Black Swan. The record label's name was said to be a tribute to opera singer Elizabeth Taylor Greenfield, who was known to her fans as the Black Swan.

Pace's company made history as the first African-American-owned record label. His board of directors was impressive and included his former professor W. E. B. Du Bois, real estate tycoon John Nail, and other members of the black elite. He hired the well-known composer William Grant Still as his musical director. He even brought along Fletcher Henderson, who had worked as a song demonstrator with Pace and Handy Sheet Music, to be the company's bandleader and recording manager.

But there was more to running a successful black record label in those days. Pace had started Black Swan in the basement of his house on Striver's Row in Harlem. But making a record required studio space with the proper recording equipment and a pressing facility where the actual records could be pressed into the flat, black, disk-shaped product. Then, before the records could go to market, they had to be wrapped and packaged. In the beginning, Pace contracted many of these services to outside companies and, more often than not, it was a white company he had to approach. On one occasion, a large white-owned business heard of Pace's bid to have his records pressed at a local company. They purchased the company to prevent Pace from making records, but this didn't stop Black Swan. Pace was able to find a plant in Wisconsin that was willing to work with an African-American.

Black Swan Records ushered in the jazz and swing era with a bang. Instead of blacks singing music designed to please the tastes of white America, they created music that celebrated their own original style and rhythms. For the first time in history, music was being recorded and marketed to the African-American consumer. Black Swan became known for producing "race records." Their slogan appeared on each album cover and in every advertisement: "The Only Genuine Colored Records—Others Are Only Passing for Colored."

On one of Black Swan's first recordings in 1921, Ethel Waters sang "Down Home Blues." Pace sent his musical groups and vocalist on an extensive tour across the United States, playing in clubs and theaters in more than fifty cities. The tour, which featured Ethel Waters, Fletcher Henderson, and the Black Swan Troubadours, made Black Swan Records sales skyrocket. In its first year, the new company had earned more than $100,000! Even today, this kind of success is a difficult achievement for a new business. The company's employees, stockholders, and board of directors were elated.

By 1922, Black Swan had purchased a building on Seventh Avenue near 135th Street. Pace employed district managers in seven major cities and more than 1,000 dealers and agents in countries all over the world. With business booming, Pace needed to produce more records to fill the demand. So he joined forces with John Fletcher, a white businessman. Together they purchased a recording studio and pressing plant. African-Americans were upset by the interracial deal and believed that Pace had turned his back on his commitment to nurture an exclusively black-run enterprise.

Unfortunately, Pace's success was also his downfall. When the major record companies saw the amount of money that could be made selling records to African-Americans, they began to open their doors to black singers and musicians. These larger companies could afford to sell their records for lower prices. This greatly reduced Pace's hold on the African-American consumer market.

The final blow to Black Swan came in 1923 with the advent of radio broadcasting. According to a letter written by Pace to colleague Roi Ottley, "Radio broadcasting broke and this spelled doom for us. Immediately dealers began to cancel orders . . . records were returned, many record stores became radio stores." Pace and his new partner went from producing and selling 7,000 records a day to only 3,000 records a day. A few months later, Pace declared bankruptcy and his factory was sold to a Chicago firm. The Black Swan label was sold to Paramount Records.

Despite his ultimate financial failure, Harry Herbert Pace displayed the beauty of black music to the world. He recorded the sounds of black musicians and singers who may have otherwise remained unheard.

W. C. Handy

Musician and Composer
1873–1958

I think America concedes that [true American music] has come from the Negro. When we take these things that are our own, and develop them until they are finer things, that's pure culture. You've got to appreciate the things that come from the art of the Negro and from the heart of the man farthest down.

W. C. Handy always loved music that came from the heart. The son of a Methodist minister, he grew up listening to Negro spirituals. When W. C. Handy was just a little boy, he would go off to the riverbank and listen to the black laborers sing as they worked at the locks of the Muscle Shoals canal.

William Christopher Handy was born in 1873 in Florence, Alabama. When he told his father he wanted to be a musician, his father said that he would rather follow his son's hearse than see him become a musician. Despite these objections, Handy saved his money, bought a cornet, and left home when he was eighteen years old. He began to play with traveling shows throughout the South, and eventually became musical director of Mahara's Minstrels. By 1908, Handy had made his way to Memphis, Tennessee, where he was asked to write a campaign song for E. H. "Boss" Crump, who was running for mayor. The song, originally named "Mr. Crump," was renamed "Memphis Blues" in 1912. It was the first song to be published with "blues" in the title. People loved the sound. Over the next four years, Handy published "St. Louis Blues," "Yellow Dog Blues," "Jo Turner Blues," and "Beale Street Blues."

Handy's songs reflected his experience. He wrote "St. Louis Blues" after his band went on the road to Chicago for the World's Columbian Exposition. The quartet traveled on to St. Louis, looking for work, but found none. The group split up and Handy was left penniless and hungry on the banks of the Mississippi River. When the sun began to set, a man nearby complained, "I hate to see that evenin' sun go down." Handy knew it was because they had to sleep on the hard cobblestones that night. Those words became the first line of Handy's most popular song, "St. Louis Blues."

Handy later formed another group, the Memphis Orchestra, and recorded "Livery Stable Blues" in 1919. Then, in 1920, he moved to New York City and founded a publishing and sheet music company with Harry Herbert Pace. Handy and Pace wrote songs and published them in sheet music form. White record-company executives would come and listen to the songs and purchase whatever suited their tastes. In 1921, Harry Pace

W. C. Handy and the Memphis Blues Band in November 1919

left the partnership and started the Pace Phonograph Corporation, which produced the Black Swan record label.

Handy tried his hand at the record business as well and started the Handy Record Company in 1922. But the company folded without making any records.

In 1926, W. C. Handy published his first book, *Blues Anthology,* and toured with Jelly Roll Morton. By this time, "St. Louis Blues" and "Beale Street Blues" had become blues classics. Handy wrote new music constantly —jazz, ragtime, spirituals, and of course, blues. Harlem Renaissance writers of the 1920s such as James Weldon Johnson, Claude McKay, Zora Neale Hurston, and Langston Hughes were committed to honoring the folk language or dialect of black people in their writing. Handy liked to write his songs in dialect too. "I wrote in Negro dialect to preserve something that I think is at times more beautiful than pure English—the way the Negro used to sing spirituals," he once explained.

Throughout the 1930s, Handy traveled with several orchestras. He worked with Clarence Davis and played at the Apollo Theatre with violinist Billy Butler and his orchestra. In 1943, Handy was blinded in an accident, but he did not stop working. He wrote and published music in Braille and continued to tour with other groups.

During his career, Handy wrote and arranged more than 150 songs. He also published his autobiography, *Father of the Blues,* in 1941 and another book, *Treasury of the Blues* in 1949. His hometown of Florence, Alabama, was so proud of his accomplishments in jazz and blues that they erected a life-size statue of him in the center of town, named a school in his honor, and started an annual, weeklong W. C. Handy Music Festival. Memphis, often thought of as the Home of the Blues, named a square and a theater in honor of Handy.

W. C. Handy died in 1958 in New York City. The log cabin along the Tennessee River where he was born is now a museum full of memorabilia that also houses a black heritage library. He was inducted into Alabama's Music Hall of Fame in 1987 and is remembered today as the Father of the Blues.

Fletcher Henderson

Music Arranger, Orchestra Leader, and Pianist
1897–1952

Fletcher Henderson headed for New York in 1920 to look for work as a chemist. As fate would have it, no one would hire a black chemist. Fortunately, he was also a skilled piano player and had little trouble finding a job as a musician.

Fletcher was born in Cuthbert, Georgia, in 1897, and began playing the piano when he was six years old. His father was a high school principal and his mother taught classical piano. Fletcher's parents, like many middle-class and upper-class blacks of that era, looked down on those music forms created by African-Americans such as spirituals, blues, and jazz. Despite his parent's views, however, Fletcher not only came to appreciate all these music forms but actually shaped the jazz music style that came to be known as swing. People wanted music they could move to, and swing was exactly that.

Henderson played piano to earn extra money while attending Atlanta University. In New York, he found work as a music demonstrator for the Harry Pace & W. C. Handy Sheet Music Company. It was after he left Pace & Handy that his career as an arranger and bandleader began to take off. Henderson took a job with Harry Pace's new record label, Black Swan, the first—and the only—African-American-owned record label in the United States in the 1920s.

In 1921, Henderson met singer Ethel Waters. This event marked the beginning of Black Swan's and Fletcher Henderson's success. According to Henderson, "I was walking along 135th Street in Harlem one night, and there, in a basement, singing with all her heart, was Ethel. I had her come down and cut two sides—"Down Home Blues" and "Oh Daddy"—that became such hits that we were made." Henderson and the Black Swan Troubadours toured with Ethel Waters throughout America. The tour was such a success that Black Swan's record sales soared to an all-time high. The group received rave reviews. The *Wilmington Dispatch* in North Carolina stated, "Ethel Waters and her jazz masters have come and gone but their memory will linger for months. The Black Swan Troubadours played an engagement at the Academy of Music last night and were so much better than had been expected the crowd was left wide-eyed and gasping with astonishment and delight." Henderson also organized a band for Bessie Smith and thirty other blues singers during the 1920s.

Henderson began to take on the additional responsibility of arranging.

The Fletcher Henderson Orchestra

As arranger, he decided how the songs would be played—for instance, when a saxophone solo would be performed, when a singer would hit the high note, or when the song would slow down or speed up. Everything about how the music was played was under his control. At a time when most bands consisted of seven or eight members, Henderson was the first jazz musician to organize a "big band" or orchestra. Some bandleaders believed that the best way to control the sound of a large band was to insist members play the song exactly as it was written. In Henderson's orchestras, however, the band members had freedom to add their individual styles to the performance. And this free expression created the unique sound of swing.

Swing was like a tonic for life. Few could resist this music that made people want to dance. Henderson's bands were known throughout clubs in Harlem and drew both white and black audiences. He played at the famed Cotton Club, on Broadway at Club Alabam, at the Roseland Ballroom, and later, at the Savoy. Henderson had an ear for talent and was known for showcasing and jump-starting the careers of some of America's best-known singers and musicians. In 1924, he hired trumpeter Louis Armstrong, with whom he recorded the hit "Sugar Foot Stomp," among other popular tunes. After Armstrong played as lead soloist with the Fletcher Henderson orchestra at the Roseland Ballroom, Henderson's orchestra became the most popular dance band in New York.

As Henderson gained more experience as an arranger, he began to develop the style that became his signature. His arrangements were the standard that other bandleaders tried to duplicate. White bandleader Benny Goodman stated, "Fletcher's ideas were far ahead of anyone else." When Henderson ran into financial trouble, he sold some of his best arrangements to Goodman, who became known as the King of Swing using Henderson's style. In 1939, an African-American musician had never before appeared onstage with a white orchestra. Henderson was the first. He joined Goodman for a few years as pianist and staff arranger. But Henderson was used to leading his own bands. Eventually, he left Goodman and put together another orchestra of his own.

In 1950, Henderson had a severe stroke that left him paralyzed and unable to play piano. He died in New York City in 1952. Fletcher Henderson's "big band swing" won the hearts of many Harlem elite who had previously ignored jazz. For the first time, a musical form crossed the boundaries of race and class. Today, many critics consider Fletcher the original King of Swing.

Louis "Satchmo" Armstrong

Composer, Trumpeter, and Singer
1901–1971

"My whole life, my soul, my whole spirit is to blow that horn," Louis Armstrong told his doctor when he refused to cancel a concert appearance in 1971—the year he died. Louis Armstrong dedicated his entire life to music, traveling around the world to perform an estimated 300 days a year. He simply loved to entertain. He once said, "the music ain't worth nothing if you can't lay it on the public."

Louis Daniel Armstrong was born in New Orleans, Louisiana, on July 4, 1901, to Mayanne and William Armstrong. Louis's father left when he was still a baby. Louis lived with his mother and sister in a two-room house in Jane Alley, in New Orleans. As a young boy, Louis loved to sing. He and three other boys from his neighborhood formed a quartet and sang on the street corner for money.

At the age of twelve, Louis was arrested for firing a gun in the street on New Year's Eve. He was sent to the Colored Waifs' Home for Boys where he lived for two years. During his stay at the boys' home, Louis learned to play the cornet and became the leader of the Waifs' Home Band. Released from the home when he was fourteen years old, Louis took odd jobs selling coal and newspapers and unloading boats. Many nights he would sit outside nightclubs to hear the bands play.

Louis learned another way to play the cornet from one of the best trumpeters in New Orleans—Joe "King" Oliver. Joe was like a father to Louis. He gave Louis his first cornet. By 1917, Armstrong was playing in a band with his mentor in the nightclubs of Storyville, New Orleans. Although he had only a fifth-grade education, Armstrong was a fast learner. His incredible skills as a cornet player earned him a spot in pianist Fate Marable's band in St. Louis. Marable's group was the regular entertainment for the Strekfus Mississippi River Boat lines. When the boats left from New Orleans, Louis played there as well.

In 1919, Louis Armstrong married Daisy Parker. They returned to New Orleans in 1921, where he played for Zutty Singleton's Trio, the Allen Brass Band, Papa Celestin's Tuxedo Orchestra, and the Silver Leaf Band. The following year, he received a telegram from King Oliver offering him a spot playing second cornet in his new Creole Jazz Band.

Armstrong packed his bags for Chicago, where his career took off. Armstrong was no ordinary cornet player—he was extraordinary. The southernflavored, Dixieland brand of jazz was a hit in Chicago. In the spirit of the Harlem Renaissance, Chicago became a hot spot for good jazz, and musicians from the South moved north to be part of the evolution of this new music form.

While playing with King Oliver's Creole Jazz Band, Armstrong recorded thirty-seven songs. He also met pianist and arranger Lillian "Lil" Hardin, who played with the band. Armstrong divorced his first wife and married Lil in 1924. At the same time, Fletcher Henderson was making big band dance music (later known as "swing") popular in New York. As the Harlem Renaissance gained momentum in the mid-1920s, artists of all kinds—musicians, singers, fine artists, and writers were sharing information and supporting one another's efforts. Henderson knew New Yorkers would welcome the new Chicago jazz sound, blended with swing. So he asked Armstrong to join the Black Swan Troubadours as lead trumpeter. Armstrong left for New York immediately. In New York, he recorded "Shanghai Shuffle," "Go 'Long Mule," "Copenhagen," and "Sugar Foot Stomp," which were all hits on the Black Swan record label. He also had the opportunity to play on Bessie Smith's legendary recording of "St. Louis Blues."

In 1925, Armstrong returned to Chicago and joined his wife Lil's band, which played at Dreamland. Shortly afterward, he started his own bands—the Hot Fives and later the Hot Sevens. Hot Five was also the name of his record label, which started recording songs that same year. The Hot Fives was exclusively a recording band and never played live, but their records are still considered among the great jazz classics. Armstrong worked year-round, performing with his own band, and with Carroll Dickenson's Orchestra and Clarence Jones's band, among others. By 1929, Armstrong was a major star.

Louis Armstrong was not only a great musician; he was a great jazz singer. He was one of the first to do "scat singing," a technique that would

Hot Chocolates *band*

make future jazz vocalists such as Ella Fitzgerald, Betty Carter, and Al Jarreau famous. Armstrong's warm, bubbly personality made his audiences feel special. When he blew his horn, people looked on in amazement as his cheeks filled with air and tripled in size. As a result, he was given the nickname "Satchel Mouth," or "Satchmo" for short.

In 1929, he toured with the black revue *Hot Chocolates* and even worked again with Fletcher Henderson. The following year, he moved to California and formed Louis Armstrong and his Sebastian New Cotton Club Orchestra for the opening of the West Coast version of the famed club. In 1931,

Armstrong went on another tour. He planned to give a free concert in his hometown of New Orleans for his African-American fans. But a white radio announcer refused to announce it, and the show had to be canceled.

In 1936, Armstrong published his autobiography, *Swing That Music.* He divorced Lil and shortly afterward began a tour of England. In 1938, he married Alpha Smith. In 1942, he divorced Alpha and married Lucille Wilson, with whom he remained for the rest of his life. The Armstrongs bought a home in Corona, Queens, New York, where he died in his sleep in 1971.

Armstrong performed all around the world. He toured throughout the United States and Hawaii, Africa, Asia, Europe, and South America. In 1964, his recording of "Hello Dolly" topped the *Billboard* charts, replacing the Beatles song "I Want to Hold Your Hand." At the age of sixty-two, he was the oldest musician in history to have a number-one song. That same year, Armstrong won a Grammy Award for "Hello Dolly." Louis Armstrong's music is enjoyed by people of all races and nationalities in countries around the globe.

Composer and conductor Leonard Bernstein declared, "Every time this man puts a trumpet to his lips, even if it is to only practice three notes, he does it with his whole soul." Armstrong's natural talent inspired the music of jazz masters such as Duke Ellington, Miles Davis, and Wynton Marsalis.

Ethel Waters

Singer and Actress
1896–1977

Ethel Waters was born in 1896 in Chester, Pennsylvania, to a teenage mother and grew up in the slums of Philadelphia. Ethel always loved to perform. When she was just a little girl, she sang at church. Ethel described her younger days as wild, claiming that she was often on her own and raised herself. By the time she became a teenager, she was known for her "hip shimmy shake." In 1911, on Halloween night, Ethel and her friends attended an amateur talent night to celebrate her birthday. On a dare, Ethel took the stage in her Halloween mask and sang W. C. Handy's "St. Louis Blues" to a packed house. Ethel stated, "They raised such a ruckus that the manager gave me first prize and a steady job."

By 1917, Waters toured with black vaudeville as both a singer and a dancer. Her stage character, named Sweet Mama Stringbean—because Waters was tall and thin—was a hit with vaudeville audiences. After her vaudeville tour was over, in 1919, Waters moved to New York. There she made her first record on the Cardinal label with "The New York Glide" and "At the New Jump Steady Ball." Then she met Fletcher Henderson, the bandleader and recording manager for the Black Swan record company, the first African-American-owned record label. There are three versions of how Black Swan discovered Waters's talent. Fletcher Henderson said he discovered Waters in a Harlem basement club, and Harry Pace, Black Swan's owner, said he discovered Waters in Atlantic City. Waters's version of her first meeting at Black Swan is as follows: "I found Fletcher Henderson sitting behind a desk and looking very prissy and important. . . . There was much discussion of whether I should sing popular or 'cultural' numbers. They finally decided on popular, and I asked one hundred dollars for making the record. I was still getting only thirty-five dollars a week. So one hundred dollars seemed quite a lump sum to me."

Waters received her $100 and Fletcher Henderson put together a band called the Black Swan Troubadours especially for her. Her first record, featuring "Down Home Blues" and "Oh Daddy," sold 500,000 copies in only six months. According to Waters, her hit "got Black Swan out of the red." Later that year, Waters, Henderson, and the Black Swan Troubadours began a tour of fifty-three cities in the United States. Her performances received rave reviews. On January 7, 1922, the *New York Age* reported, "Ms. Waters and her band has [sic] been making a hit in every theatre she has

The Blackbirds of 1930

played since beginning her tour." When the tour was about to reach its southern leg, a few of the musicians refused to go. In 1922, the lynching of blacks was still a big problem in the south. Marcus Garvey's United Negro Improvement Association (UNIA) marched with the NAACP and the YMCA to support the federal anti-lynching bill, but Waters did not want her black fans in the South to suffer because of the political climate. She refused to be discouraged by racism. The musicians were replaced and the tour went on as scheduled.

Black Swan Records went bankrupt in 1924, and by 1925, Waters had signed with Columbia Records. Fans loved her crystal-clear soprano voice.

Her long dangling earrings became her trademark look. She had fans across the country who continued to want more, and Waters responded, recording fifty hit songs in only a few years. Everything Waters sang turned into a hit.

In the late 1920s, all-black musical revues were popular, featuring songs and music written and performed by African-Americans. This was at the height of the Harlem Renaissance and was a great source of pride for black people. In 1927, Waters starred in *Africana*. The following year, she appeared with Bill "Bojangles" Robinson, in the hit *Blackbirds*. In 1931, she was also in *Rhapsody in Black*. Next, Waters went on to film. She appeared in *On with the Show* and in *Check and Double Check*, with Amos 'n' Andy and Duke Ellington.

One of the star's most memorable nights occurred in 1933. Waters was performing at Harlem's famed Cotton Club, with Duke Ellington and George Dewey Washington, and introduced a new song, "Stormy Weather," written for her by composer Harold Arlen. Producers had little interest in the tune until Waters delivered it to the cheering crowd. That night, "Stormy Weather" became Waters's theme song. When composer Irving Berlin heard Waters sing the tune he signed her for his upcoming revue *As Thousands Cheer*.

By the late 1930s, she was on Broadway, starring in *Cabin in the Sky*, *Mamba's Daughters*, and *At Home Abroad*. She was nominated for an Oscar for Best Supporting Actress in *Pinky*. In 1950, she won the New York Drama Critics Award for Best Actress in *Member of the Wedding*. She was the first African-American to star in a radio show.

About 1959, Waters shifted her focus to religion and toured with evangelist Billy Graham. In her autobiography *His Eye Is on the Sparrow* (1951), she details her rise to fame. In 1972, she wrote her second autobiography *To Me It's Wonderful*. Waters died in 1977 at the age of eighty in Chatsworth, California.

Bessie Smith

Singer
1894?–1937

Blues legend Bessie Smith was born at a time when birth records of African-Americans, especially those born in the South, were not properly documented and maintained. She was born sometime between 1894 and 1900 in Chattanooga, Tennessee. The Smiths were very poor and lived in what Bessie referred to as "a ramshackle cabin." Her father, a Baptist minister, died when Bessie was only nine years old, and her mother was left to care for six children alone. She worked as a street performer, barely getting by on whatever money passersby offered.

Bessie's mentor was none other than the Mother of the Blues—Gertrude "Ma" Rainey. In 1912, Bessie toured with the Moses Stokes Show as a dancer and singer. Ma Rainey had stopped in Chattanooga with her revue *The Rabbit Foot Minstrels* and just happened to see Bessie perform. When she heard Smith's young, soulful voice, she decided to take Bessie under her wing. Bessie traveled with Ma and her revue until 1915. Then she joined the Theater Owners Booking Association (TOBA) and performed with the black vaudeville circuit. Vaudeville was a popular form of traveling show that featured short comedy routines, dance, and musical acts. The black vaudevillians performed comedy and musical acts with such stage names as Butterbeans and Susie, Bojangles, Black Patti and the Troubadours, Pigmeat, Sweet Mama Stringbean, Moms, Hamtree, the Whitman Sisters, Stump and Stumpy, Miller and Lyles, and Kid and Coot. These talented actors, singers, dancers, and musicians received low pay and sometimes no pay at all. They lived out of a suitcase traveling from city to city, usually by train, at a time when many hotels and restaurants refused to serve African-Americans. But those who performed for TOBA loved the stage enough to keep going when money was tight and times were hard.

By 1920, vaudeville was no longer popular, but during Prohibition, Smith was still able to get plenty of work in the speakeasies (private night-clubs that sold liquor illegally). These establishments made lots of money and employed regular entertainment for their guests. Audiences loved the way Smith sang the blues. She was known for her temper and often got into fights after drinking too much gin. The anger, pain, and humor that she brought to her songs earned her the title Empress of the Blues. Her voice was so rich and so deep that to hear her sing you would believe she had lived every word of her "bluesy" tales.

In 1923, Smith moved to New York City and was offered a contract with Columbia to make her first recording, which featured "Down-Hearted Blues" and "Gulf Coast Blues." The record was a hit and sold more than 750,000 copies. Smith was officially a star. She sang with all the great musicians and orchestras—Sidney Bechet, Joe Smith, Louis Armstrong, Fletcher Henderson, James Johnson, and Benny Goodman. Bessie Smith became one of the highest-paid black entertainers, making between $1,500 and $2,000 a week. Although the blues was popular with both black and white audiences, many leaders of the Harlem Renaissance, Du Bois included, felt that it was a low-class musical form. They urged blacks to excel in the "respectable" form of classical music. The younger generation rejected this idea and proclaimed their pride in the music of the "common" black American. Langston Hughes even wrote, "Let the blare of Negro jazz bands and the bellowing voice of Bessie Smith singing the blues penetrate the closed ears of the colored near-intellectuals, until they listen and perhaps understand."

Bessie Smith sang every brand of blues imaginable—reckless blues, sobbin' hearted blues, yellow dog blues, house rent blues, Nashville woman blues, jailhouse blues, and more. Her biggest hit—a song by W. C. Handy that she recorded in 1925 with Louis Armstrong—was "St. Louis Blues." In 1929, W. C. Handy and Kenneth Adams wrote a short film based on the "St. Louis Blues." Handy loved Smith's memorable version of his hit song and asked her to star in the film, which boasted an all-black cast and some of the best bands in the business. That same year the stock market crashed. Many people lost their life's savings and had a real reason to sing the blues. When Smith sang her hit "Nobody Knows You When You're Down and Out," she made it sound as if it was her own life story. Three years later, America's desire for the blues faded, and Columbia dropped Bessie from their label because of slipping sales.

Smith updated her classical blues style to swing, the latest music craze. She was on her way to a comeback in 1937, when she died in an automobile accident in Clarksdale, Mississippi. Like many extraordinary people of the Harlem Renaissance, Smith's success paved the way for those entertainers who followed. She continues to be admired by young performers and is still remembered as the Empress of the Blues.

Bill "Bojangles" Robinson

Dancer and Entertainer
1878–1949

It was a time when the achievements of one black person felt like the achievement of all black Americans. A smooth, smiling, dapper young man danced his way into American history, and the hearts of black America danced with him.

The first of Maxwell and Maria Robinson's two sons was born on May 25, 1878, in Richmond, Virginia. They named him Luther, but he didn't like that name. He suggested to his younger brother,

Bill, that they swap names. When Bill declined, Luther persuaded him with his fists. Thus, Luther Robinson became Bill Robinson.

Bill's father was a machine-shop worker, and his mother sang in a choir. Unfortunately, the Robinsons did not live to see their son's success. They both died when Bill was still a baby. Bill and his younger brother were taken in and raised by their grandmother.

At the age of six, Bill danced for pennies on the streets and in saloons. Before he was eight years old, he ran away to Washington D.C., and got a job as a stable boy at a racetrack.

Bill loved to watch the dancers in the traveling minstrel shows. He spent hours learning their steps and making up new ones. Two years later, he toured with Mayme Remington's Dance Troupe. Dancing was like breathing for Bill—natural. The music seemed to tell his feet what to do. In 1892, the twelve-year-old polished veteran joined the South before the War, a traveling minstrel company.

Through constant practice and experimentation, Robinson developed his own unique style, adding new elements to the art of tap dancing. In its early days, tap dancing was done in a flat-footed style. By dancing on the balls of his feet instead, Robinson was able to add faster rhythms and more excitement. When he was balancing "up on his toes," Robinson could use more intricate footwork. Everywhere he danced, people were amazed by his new style.

It was in Chicago in 1908 that Robinson met the respected and successful vaudeville agent Marty Forkins. Under Forkins's career guidance, Robinson began working as a solo act in nightclubs. His earnings climbed to $3,500 a week. Robinson's fame continued to grow as he won critical acclaim in a series of Broadway musicals and thrilled audiences with his own invention, the "stair dance."

Until he was fifty years old, Robinson had performed only for black audiences. Then, in 1928, Lew Leslie produced *Blackbirds of 1928.* It was Robinson's first all-black review specifically made for white audiences. He starred in 518 performances of *Blackbirds,* and the white audiences loved it. Then came *Brown Buddies of 1930,* followed by another run of *Blackbirds* in 1933.

Celebrities and political figures made Robinson an honorary mayor of Harlem. He received a lifetime membership in police associations and fraternal orders. Robinson was even named mascot of the New York Giants baseball team.

Robinson had a special style that audiences just loved. Instead of the common, jerky style of the jitterbug, Robinson always played it cool. His upper body stayed calm and controlled. He relied on his facial expressions and swiftly tapping feet to carry the scene.

After 1930, the demand for black reviews dwindled, but Robinson remained popular with white audiences, making fourteen motion pictures in ten years. Robinson made movies with RKO Pictures, Twentieth-Century Fox, and Paramount. He appeared with child star Shirley Temple in four musicals.

Robinson was rarely able to break away from the stereotyped roles created by Hollywood writers. Notable exceptions were *Hooray for Love* (1935) and *One Mile from Heaven* (1937). The 1943 musical *Stormy Weather* paired Robinson as the romantic lead with Lena Horne, one of the first movies that marked Hollywood's relaxation of a previous ban on blacks in leading romantic roles. It was a definite stride forward for blacks to be portrayed as feeling, loving human beings.

After spending nine years away, Bill "Bojangles" Robinson returned to the stage in a jazz version of the operetta *The Hot Mikado.* The show was produced for the 1939–1940 New York World's Fair. The production and Bill's performance were the talk of the fair.

The Big Broadcast of 1936

After 1940, Robinson gave only occasional live performances, but he continued to dance even in his sixties. To demonstrate his incredible versatility, he once danced in front of a class for one hour without repeating a single step. Robinson insisted that his feet responded directly to the music; he didn't even have to think about it.

To celebrate turning sixty years old, Robinson danced sixty blocks from north of Columbus Circle in New York City down Broadway and into the theater where he was performing that evening.

Bill "Bojangles" Robinson died on November 25, 1949. He was seventy-one years old. His coffin lay in state at the Harlem armory, and 60,000 people walked slowly past to pay their last respects. Politicians and show-business stars, both black and white, stood up to speak at his funeral and paid homage to this wonderful entertainer who danced across color lines in tap shoes.

Charles S. Gilpin

Actor
1878–1930

Charles S. Gilpin was born in 1878 in the Jackson Ward section of Richmond, Virginia. At the age of twelve, he decided to drop out of St. Francis School for Catholic Colored Children. He became a printer's apprentice for the *Richmond Planet* newspaper, but later decided to pursue his true love, the theater.

Charles began singing at saloons and theaters in his hometown and worked as a temporary performer when traveling shows came to Richmond. In the early 1890s, Charles moved to Philadelphia with his mother. There he joined and toured with the Williams and Walker Vaudeville Company—singing, dancing, and performing a comedy routine. He also toured with the Perkus and Davis Great Southern Minstrel Barn Storming Aggregation. When his tour ended and the company closed, Charles gave up on his dream of acting, at least for a while. He got married and settled down into a job as a barber. However, when the opportunity presented itself, Gilpin added his deep baritone vocals to the Canadian Jubilee Singers and became one of the first members of the Pekin Stock Company in Chicago.

In 1914, Gilpin met Anita Bush, who ran one of the first African-American theater companies. Bush asked him to join her company and play the male lead in *The Girl at the Fort.* The Anita Bush Company eventually took up residence in New York's Lafayette Theater and became the "most stylish black showplace in Harlem." When Bush sold the company, Gilpin became a founding member of the Lafayette Players.

W. E. B. Du Bois stated that the Negro theater must be "about us, by us, for us, and near us." Charles Gilpin's Lafayette Players, among other groups, met all of those requirements except one. In those early days, there were no plays "written" by African-Americans. But there were many black theater groups. Harlem alone had the Krigwa Players, the Harlem Experimental Group, the Utopia Players, the Harlem Community Players, and the Negro Art Theater. There was also the Karamu Theater of Cleveland, the Pekin Theater in Chicago, and others.

Though blacks had a chance to sing, dance, and act in vaudeville shows, the goal in vaudeville was usually to make audiences laugh. One other option for black actors was the minstrel shows, which perpetuated racist stereotypes of shuffling "darkies" who sang and danced their troubles away. Black theater groups gave their actors an opportunity to test their wings with dramatic performances. In fact, these groups were just about the only training ground for black actors in those days.

Between his acting jobs, Charles Gilpin had every side job imaginable. He was an elevator operator at Macy's, a porter, even a trainer for prize-fighters. In 1919, he got his first Broadway role in John Drinkwater's *Abraham Lincoln*. Gilpin played Custis, a former slave and minister. His performance was so outstanding that he was asked to play the starring role in Eugene O'Neill's *The Emperor Jones* in 1920. Gilpin was the first African-American to star in a play in an all-white theater. The play opened at the Provincetown Theater in Greenwich Village, New York, and played on Broadway before touring several other U.S. cities. *The Emperor Jones* received rave reviews in the actor's hometown of Richmond, Virginia, and just about everywhere it was performed. At the height of his fame, Charles Gilpin was invited to the White House. He received the NAACP Spingarn Medal, and he was hailed in *New Republic* as one of the greatest American actors.

But Gilpin's success declined almost as fast as it began. O'Neill's play included racial slurs that made Charles Gilpin uncomfortable. He began to complain, which only angered Eugene O'Neill. Gilpin began to change his lines despite O'Neill's objections. He also began to drink heavily, and it showed on stage. So when *The Emperor Jones* was set to open in 1924 in London, O'Neill decided to drop Gilpin and use another black actor—Paul Robeson.

Despite his increasing problem with alcohol, Gilpin continued to act in other plays and was committed to supporting the black theater. He donated large sums of money to Cleveland's Karamu Theater. The Karamu Players even changed their name to the Gilpin Players in his honor. Gilpin starred in the Colored Players Film Corporation's *Ten Nights in a Barroom*. But efforts to revive his career did not work.

By 1929, Gilpin had become ill and lost his voice. He died in 1930, at his Eldridge Park, New Jersey, home, at the age of fifty-one. Despite their difficulties, Eugene O'Neill continued to praise Charles Gilpin: "As I look back now on all my work, I can honestly say there was only one actor who carried every notion of a character I had in my mind. That actor was Charles Gilpin."

Paul Leroy Robeson

Scholar, Athlete, Actor, Singer, and Political Activist
1898–1976

The artist must elect to fight for freedom or for slavery. . . . I have made my choice.

These were the words of Paul Robeson, who like his parents, believed in freedom. His father, William Robeson, bravely escaped from slavery using the Underground Railroad at the age of fifteen. His mother, Maria, had been a free abolitionist from one of the oldest African-American abolitionist families.

Paul Leroy Robeson was born in Princeton, New Jersey, in 1898. His father, a Presbyterian minister, was known for speaking out against injustice. This was frowned upon by the church authorities and Reverend Robeson was forced to resign. As a result, he had to drive a coach and haul ashes to earn a living. Paul's mother, a schoolteacher, died tragically when he was only six years old. Her clothing caught fire while she was standing over a coal stove.

Paul's father joined the African Methodist Episcopal (AME) Zion Church and moved his five children first to Westerfield, New Jersey, and then, two years later, to Somerville, New Jersey. There Paul attended Somerville High School, where he excelled as a student, speaker, and athlete. One of a dozen African-Americans out of a total of 200 students, Paul managed to become quite popular. Although his talents made him welcome in certain white circles, he was never fully accepted because of his race.

In 1915, Robeson won a four-year scholarship to Rutgers College. At Rutgers he became both a star athlete and a scholar. At six feet, two inches and 190 pounds, he was a superman in every sport, winning fifteen varsity letters in baseball, basketball, football, and track. During his senior year in 1918, he was the first African-American to be chosen for the Walter Camp All-American Football Team. In his junior year, he was inducted into the Phi Beta Kappa honor society. In 1919, Robeson graduated from Rutgers as valedictorian of his class, then moved to New York to attend Columbia University Law School. He supported himself by playing professional football and tutoring his coach's son in Latin.

At Columbia, Robeson met and fell in love with Eslanda Goode, and they were married in 1921. Eslanda admired Robeson's talent as a speaker and suggested that he audition for a play at the Harlem YMCA. Robeson was offered the leading role in *Simon the Cyrenian* and hesitantly accepted. Though the play was an amateur production, it attracted people who were

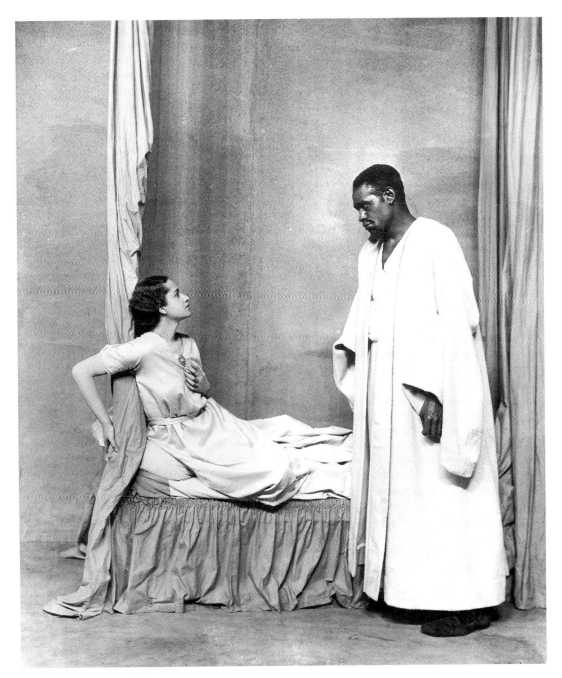

Paul Robeson as Othello

involved in professional theater. The founders of the Provincetown Play-house offered Robeson the lead in an upcoming Eugene O'Neill play, but he turned them down, recalling "I went home and forgot about the theatre, and went back the next morning to law school as if nothing had happened." The next year, he made his professional acting debut as Jim in *Taboo* at the Sam Harris Theater. And in 1922, he was offered a role in a British production of the same play, now named *Voodoo*. Each acting role he accepted led to more work as an actor, but Robeson still had his sights set on a career in law.

Robeson got his law degree in 1923 and was hired by Stotesbury and Miner, a top law firm in New York. There had never been an African-American attorney at that high-profile firm, and some of the staff resented his presence. One day a white secretary refused to take dictation from Robeson. Only a few months into his legal career, he resigned and returned to acting.

Black and white New Yorkers were abuzz in 1924 when Robeson took center stage as the lead in Eugene O'Neill's *All God's Chillun Got Wings*. The play featured a white actress in the role of Robeson's wife. This upset some members of the white community, resulting in threats of bombing and other violence. Despite the uproar, the show went on without incident. When actor Charles Gilpin was fired from the cast of *The Emperor Jones,* Robeson was asked to replace him in the leading role. The show, which had already received rave reviews for Gilpin's performance, continued to play to packed houses in the United States and London. In 1924, Robeson became a star of stage and screen. He acted in his first film, *Body and Soul,* and performed his first concert.

In 1925, Robeson was the first person to give a full concert of Negro spirituals. The concert was so successful it launched him into star status. But Robeson did not let his newfound stardom change his core beliefs. He made every attempt to maintain integrity in his work and turned down roles that stereotyped African-American people. Paul Robeson showed the world that black people were capable of great achievements in the arts. His outstanding performances were a source of great pride for Harlemites and for all African-Americans. But Robeson was frustrated by the lack of good roles for black actors. He began to see that America was not yet ready for the New Negro.

Robeson saw that the lesson he had learned as a young teen still held true—popularity does not equal full acceptance. As he toured the United States with various musical productions and plays during the Harlem Renaissance, he was often denied hotel accommodations because of his race.

Even in London, where Robeson had earned critical acclaim for his performance in the hit musical *Showboat,* he encountered racism. Eslanda and Robeson were denied entry into London's famed Savoy Grill. But it was Robeson's journeys abroad that moved him to look deeper into the roots of African culture. When he toured Vienna, Prague, and Budapest, Robeson was introduced to Romany (gypsy) folk songs. He was so taken by their similarities to black folk music that he later performed a concert that presented the musical forms together. Robeson began to study African culture and history, "trying to find an Art that is purely Negro, that is not dependent on Western and European influence." He and Eslanda also wanted to find a place that would be receptive to such an art form.

In 1933, the couple toured the Soviet Union. During the Harlem Renaissance, African-Americans were in search of a fairer political system. Some believed that the socialist system of government of the U.S.S.R. offered equal treatment to all races. During their tour, Robeson and his wife witnessed a society that had been influenced by both socialism and communism. He said, "Here for the first time in my life, I walk in full human dignity." Robeson traveled the world as a champion for freedom. He helped Max Yergan found the Council on African Affairs, an organization designed to promote Africa's self-rule and independence. And like Langston Hughes, he went to Spain to join the fight against fascism. When Robeson condemned the United States's refusal to support Spain in its fight for freedom, the U.S. government began to take notice of Robeson's newfound foreign friendships.

Despite warnings from his agent, Robeson never failed to speak his mind on racial injustice in America. In 1945, Robeson was awarded the NAACP's Spingarn Medal. In his acceptance speech, he made his feelings known about the increasing racial tensions in America, despite the full participation of African-Americans in World War II. The FBI made a report of his remarks and added the Robesons' names to the list of people suspected of being communists. The investigation ultimately led to the government taking away Robeson's passport so that he could not travel abroad for performances. They also removed his albums from stores and prevented him from performing in the United States.

With the activism and support of friends worldwide, Robeson's passport was returned, and he successfully resumed his career in 1952. In 1958, he wrote his autobiography, *Here I Stand.* Robeson died in 1976, in Philadelphia, Pennsylvania.

Paul Robeson was one of the best-loved and most respected entertainers in history. Actor Ossie Davis, a dear friend of the Robesons, described his contribution the best, "We blacks need so much to be reminded of something great. We have heroes that we worshiped and they made a great difference, like Joe Louis for example, or Marian Anderson, and to top it all, Paul Robeson. Just to look at him, to be in love with him was to be alive in a different kind of way."

James P. Johnson

Jazz Pianist and Composer
1891–1955

James P. Johnson was known as the father of stride piano. Stride is a jazz style in which the piano player keeps the melody with the right hand and plays one note and one chord, alternately, with the left. It is one of the most difficult piano-playing techniques. With fast, strong hands, amazing coordination, and technical skill, Johnson took jazz piano to a new level.

James Price Johnson was born in 1891 in New Brunswick,

New Jersey. As a young boy, James loved to "tickle the ivories" and he decided that his goal in life was to be a "tickler," a piano player. His first music teacher was his mother who taught him classical piano. His first job as a musician was at a local sporting house, where he was required to play for two hours nonstop. In 1917, he started work for the Q.R.S. Company recording piano rolls for player pianos.

During the Harlem Renaissance, rent parties (also called shouts, jumps, or struts) were a popular pastime of the same elite who claimed not to like blues or jazz. There could be a rent party any night of the week. Rent parties usually began just after midnight and cost only a quarter for admission. They were not casual affairs, however. People came dressed in their "Sunday best" or in formal attire, and Johnson was no exception. He always wore the finest clothes. In Harlem, there was an inner circle of piano players with nicknames such as Abba Labba, the Bear, and the Lion. Johnson was considered the dean of shout pianists.

Just as an athlete trains for the Olympics, Johnson worked hard in his spare time to perfect his talent. He studied blues and ragtime music, as well as traditional music theory and technique, earning a reputation as the best "piano professor" on the East Coast. In addition to rent parties, Johnson played for cabarets and toured the vaudeville circuit. He even performed the piano accompaniment on recordings for blues legends Ethel Waters, Bessie Smith, and Ida Cox.

In 1921, Johnson recorded the first jazz piano solo ever—"Carolina Shout." He became so popular that every musician who wanted to learn stride studied his technique by watching the pianola (or player piano) play his prerecorded songs. James recorded hundreds of piano rolls under his own name, a rare opportunity for African-American musicians in those days. At one point, Johnson recorded a new piano roll every other week.

Johnson also contributed to the Harlem Renaissance and to the development of jazz through teaching. Among his most famous students was Fats Waller. Fats won a talent competition playing "Carolina Shout," which he learned to play by studying Johnson's piano rolls.

The Negro musical revue was an important feature of the Harlem Renaissance. These shows were written and performed by all-black casts and drew theatergoers from both the African-American and white communities. During the 1920s, Johnson wrote eleven musical scores for such revues as *Running Wild* and *Plantation Days*. It was the 1923 musical *Running Wild* that started the dance craze called the Charleston. Based on African and Caribbean dance movements, the Charleston was a black folk dance from Charleston, South Carolina. The song that accompanied the dance, also named "The Charleston," became one of the most popular songs in American history. In addition to providing the perfect rhythms for the dance, this tune symbolized the spirit of the Roaring Twenties and is regarded as the theme song of that era.

Johnson was a versatile musician and continued to write classical music, as well. All together, he composed nineteen symphonies including *Yamecraw: A Negro Rhapsody,* performed at New York's Carnegie Hall in 1928; *Harlem Symphony,* in 1932; and a one-act blues opera *The Organizer,* in 1940, with lyrics by poet Langston Hughes. In the 1950s, Johnson began to have health problems, but he continued to perform until his death in 1955.

James P. Johnson did far more than inspire future stride pianists. His genius moved young musicians to bring something new to jazz by innovating new techniques. For example, stride was the foundation of Fats Waller's "boogie-woogie" jazz. Johnson is also credited with inspiring the work of such jazz masters as Duke Ellington and Thelonious Monk.

James Hubert "Eubie" Blake

Musician, Composer, and Performer
1883–1983

ohn Sumner Blake and Emily Johnson were not allowed to marry because they were slaves, but when the Emancipation Proclamation was signed in 1863 they became husband and wife. After several attempts at having a family, Emily gave birth to a baby boy who later become one of the greatest musical talents in history.

James Hubert "Eubie" Blake was born in 1883 in Baltimore, Maryland. His musical genius was evident when he was only four years old. While shopping with his mother, Eubie wandered into a nearby music store and began playing the organ. Emily was a religious woman who believed it was a sin not to use the gifts that God gave, so she purchased the $75 pump organ for her son and enrolled him in piano lessons with a neighborhood teacher.

Eubie loved the exciting rhythms of ragtime music, and he played the songs despite his mother's disapproval. "Get that ragtime out of my house," his mother demanded. Word of Eubie's musical gifts spread through the Baltimore neighborhood. When he was fifteen years old, the owner of a local brothel offered him a job playing in her establishment. Every night, Eubie slipped off to work, keeping his earnings and his new job a secret from his parents—at least until a church member notified Mrs. Blake of her son's new position. Though Eubie's mother strongly disapproved, she did not ask him to quit.

By 1899, Blake had begun to write music. His song "Sounds of Africa," later renamed "Charleston Rag," is considered one of the first songs to introduce the "stride" style of playing piano. Blake not only composed his own songs, he also danced. He worked as a "buck dancer" with a traveling medicine show, performed on Broadway, and played piano wherever he could find work. In 1908, he took a job as a pianist at the Goldfield Hotel in Baltimore. Blake honed his skills by watching and learning from other pianists such as Willie "the Lion" Smith, C. Luckeyeth Roberts, James P. Johnson, and Llewellyn Wilson. The following summer he began dating Avis Lee, a classical pianist, who became his wife.

In 1915, Blake joined Joe Porter's Serenaders, where he met songwriter Noble Sissle. The two discovered instantly that they worked well together. Only a few days after they met, they had written their first song, "It's All Your Fault." They took the song to actress Sophie Tucker, who was known for helping black songwriters. She liked the song so much that she used it

Noble Sissle and Eubie Blake

in her show the following night. Blake and Sissle wrote and produced their own act and toured with white vaudeville, also known as the Keith circuit. Few African-Americans performed in white vaudeville, and only one black act was allowed per show. In the days of vaudeville, both black and white entertainers often performed in blackface, but not Blake and Sissle. Audiences knew the two as the Dixie Duo.

At an NAACP fund-raiser in Philadelphia in 1920, Blake and Sissle met Flournoy Miller and Aubrey Lyles, another songwriting duo. The four teamed up and produced the first all-black Broadway musical hit, *Shuffle Along. Shuffle Along* began as a road show and made its New York debut at the 63rd Street Theatre on May 23, 1921. It was the first musical comedy to include a dramatic storyline and it revolutionized the Broadway musical. The show attracted an integrated audience, which posed a problem. In the 1920s, African-Americans were only allowed to be seated in the balcony. This kind of seating arrangement was not acceptable to the show's black producers, so they created "black" and "white" sections throughout the theater, to ensure that African-Americans could have access to the better seats.

In the 1920s, black people were never portrayed as having romantic and loving relationships onstage. Blake and Sissle boldly debuted their song "Love Will Find a Way" on opening night. While Blake played piano onstage during the romantic number, the cast stood prepared to leave the theater in case the number caused a riot among whites in the audience. To their surprise, the audience loved the song and responded with cheerful applause. The most famous song from *Shuffle Along* was Blake and Sissle's, "I'm Just Wild about Harry," which was used years later in Harry Truman's 1948 presidential campaign.

The Dixie Duo went on to write and produce the musicals *Elsie* and *Chocolate Dandies.* Blake also wrote musicals of his own, including *Swing It* and the popular *Blackbirds,* which began its long run in 1925. That same year, Blake and Sissle toured Europe and composed music for a British revue. In 1929, when Sissle decided to remain in Paris, the duo broke up.

In the 1930s, America was in the midst of the Great Depression. During this period, Blake's wife, Avis, contracted tuberculosis and died. Heartbroken and depressed, Blake took a break from the entertainment business, and everyone believed his career was over. But in 1941, when the United States entered World War II, Blake took to the stage again, traveling and performing for the U.S. troops. In 1945, he met his second wife,

Marion Tyler, who gave him a new lease on life. He enrolled in classes in music and composition at New York University in 1950 and earned his bachelor's degree at the age of sixty-seven.

In 1968, he reunited with Noble Sissle to record "86 Years of Eubie Blake." Ten years later, a successful Broadway production titled *Eubie!* celebrated the performer's life. James Hubert "Eubie" Blake wrote hundreds of songs for the stage. He once stated in an interview, "I had written about a couple of thousand pieces, but only about 350 had ever been published."

He died five days after his one hundredth birthday in 1983.

Edward Kennedy "Duke" Ellington

Composer, Pianist, and Bandleader
1899–1974

*E*dward "Duke" Ellington was the very image of the New Negro—handsome, suave, and sophisticated. He was one of the greatest composers in the history of jazz music, as well as one of the most important musicians of the twentieth century.

Edward Kennedy Ellington was born on April 29, 1899, in Washington, D.C. His parents, Daisy Kennedy Ellington and James Edward Ellington, were middle-class and made sure that he learned good manners and knew how to carry himself like a gentleman. Both of his parents had backgrounds in music, and they taught Edward about the emotional power of music. Because of his clothes, personality, and manners, one of his childhood friends gave Edward the nickname "Duke." That name fit him so well that he kept it for the rest of his life.

Duke received his first piano lessons around the age of seven. At that time, only baseball captured his interest. Later, as a teenager, Duke listened to ragtime musicians around Washington. While vacationing with his mother in Philadelphia, he heard Harvey Brooks, a popular piano player. Duke learned some of Harvey's techniques and was inspired to play more. "When I got home I had a real yearning to play . . . after hearing him I said to myself, 'Man you're going to have to do it.'"

Oliver "Doc" Perry and Louis Brown taught Ellington to read music and improve his piano skills. Soon Ellington was playing ragtime music for parties, clubs, and cafes around Washington. He formed his first dance-band—the Duke's Serenaders—in 1917. Acting as his own booking agent, Ellington was very successful at getting jobs for the band to play at private dances, embassy parties, and clubs throughout Washington and in nearby Virginia. Ellington married Edna Thompson, and they had a son, Mercer Kennedy Ellington, born on March 11, 1919.

In 1923, Ellington decided to leave the steady work in Washington for a chance to make it big in New York City. He changed the name of the band to the Washingtonians, and they played at the Hollywood Club in Manhattan (later named the Kentucky Club).

Ellington wanted his band to really stand out among the jazz bands playing for the rent parties and clubs of New York City. Unlike other band-leaders of his day, Ellington wrote and arranged the music for his band. He looked for musicians who could add a unique sound to his band, and then wrote music that suited the strengths of each instrument and each band

Duke Ellington and his orchestra

member. For that reason, musicians tended to stay with Ellington for decades. The trumpeter James "Bubber" Miley brought his signature "muted horn" style of playing. It became known as the "jungle sound" and added to the popularity of Ellington's band.

In 1924, the group made their first record. It had "Choo Choo" on one side, and "Rainy Nights" on the flip side. The band's popularity soared. They played New York hot spots like the Exclusive Club, Ciro's, the Plantation Club, and such prestigious, whites-only clubs as Connie's Inn and the Cotton Club.

By the mid-1920s, the little band from Washington had grown to twelve members and was known as the Duke Ellington Orchestra. Ellington experimented with using a singer's voice like an instrument, singing notes as sounds but not using real words, as in "Creole Love Call" recorded in 1927. At times, his musicians even made their instruments sound like talking voices. "Tricky Sam" Nanton, for example, was known for making his trombone sound like a person speaking.

Ellington continued to try new approaches in writing and performing his music. Because of his innovative sounds, the band's popularity continued to grow and led to the Duke Ellington Orchestra becoming the house band for the Cotton Club. Radio broadcasts from the club brought them national attention and more fame. The unique Ellington sound was at its best in songs such as "Black and Tan Fantasy" (1927), "The Mooche" (1928), and "Mood Indigo" (1930). These recordings along with the broadcasts from the Cotton Club brought the Duke Ellington Orchestra world renown.

The orchestra left the Cotton Club in 1931 on an extended tour of the United States and Europe. But even a hectic touring schedule could not keep Ellington from constantly experimenting and improving on his signature sound. By 1932, Ellington had fourteen members in his orchestra and led the way from 1920s hot jazz to 1930s swing music. Ellington's hit song "It Don't Mean a Thing If It Ain't Got That Swing" (1931) became the defining song of the swing dance craze of the 1930s.

It was Ellington's willingness to change and adapt his sound to the spirit of the times, while still being true to his own musical vision, that kept the Duke Ellington Orchestra at the forefront of jazz. Ellington composed some 2,000 works in his lifetime. Some of them were musical comedies. Others were instrumentals for ballets. Ellington even wrote music for an opera and for motion pictures. He won eleven Grammy Awards and received nineteen honorary degrees, including doctorates from Howard and Yale

Universities. He also received the highest honors that can be awarded to a civilian in America and in France—the Presidential Medal of Freedom (1969) and the Legion of Honor (1973) respectively.

For fifty years, Ellington led his band, always striving to keep his sound fresh and new. He carried the jazz music of the New Negro across America and to sixty five other countries around the world. When Edward Kennedy "Duke" Ellington died of cancer in 1974, his son, Mercer K. Ellington, stepped forward to lead the band and to preserve the sound that Duke had made world famous.

The spirit of the Jazz Age, the hope and self-pride that characterized the Harlem Renaissance, is heard in every note of Duke Ellington's music. Today, a hundred years after his birth, Ellington's musical legacy lives on and continues to be played, enriching the lives of Americans and of people all over the world.

Getting the Word Out:
Publications of the Harlem Renaissance

Getting the word out was the task of newspapers and literary magazines during the Harlem Renaissance. These publications brought the opinions, feelings, and intentions of the New Negro to the public. They not only included essays, poetry, and prose but they also showcased the art of the time and portrayed the powerful themes of racism and the push for African cultural pride.

Black-owned newspapers across the country, such as the *Amsterdam News,* the *Chicago Defender,* the *Pittsburgh Courier,* and the *Boston Guardian* spread news of the outstanding achievements of the Harlem community. Though there were many black-owned newspapers, there were only a handful of black-owned literary magazines and journals to provide an outlet for the poetry, prose, and art of African-Americans. The *Crisis, Opportunity,* the *Messenger,* and the *Negro World* were considered the top four black publications of the era.

THE CRISIS

A RECORD OF THE DARKER RACES

Volume One   NOVEMBER, 1910   Number One

Edited by W. E. BURGHARDT DU BOIS, with the co-operation of Oswald Garrison Villard, J. Max Barber, Charles Edward Russell, Kelly Miller, W. S. Braithwaite and M. D. Maclean.

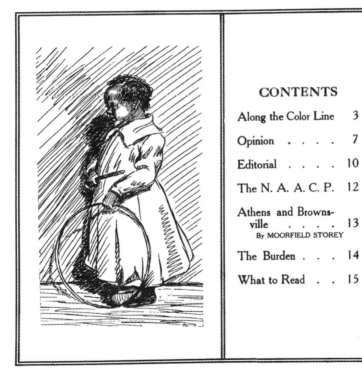

CONTENTS

PUBLISHED MONTHLY BY THE

National Association for the Advancement of Colored People

AT TWENTY VESEY STREET   NEW YORK CITY

ONE DOLLAR A YEAR   TEN CENTS A COPY

The cover of the first issue of The Crisis

African-Americans were otherwise dependent on white editors of mainstream magazines to take interest in their work. Getting published in these magazines was no easy task, but it was possible. White-run magazines such as *Harper's* and *Vanity Fair* featured the art of Aaron Douglas and the poetry of Langston Hughes, among others. This was an important development because it made white Americans aware of the art, culture, and concerns of the New Negro.

The major literary journals and newspapers of the Harlem Renaissance included:

The Crisis: A Record of the Darker Races. The official magazine of the National Association for the Advancement of Colored People (NAACP), edited by W. E. B. Du Bois and literary editor Jessie Redmon Fauset. The goal of the *Crisis* was to make African-Americans aware of political and social issues. The *Crisis* had an ongoing antilynching message. Every issue reported the number of violent incidents against African-Americans.

Opportunity: A Journal of Negro Life. The official magazine of the National Urban League. The magazine's editor, Charles Spurgeon Johnson, organized *Opportunity's* literary contests to honor the talented writers of the Harlem Renaissance. Large cash prizes helped support the work of prizewinners such as Zora Neale Hurston, Langston Hughes, and Countee Cullen. Executive secretary of the Urban League Eugene Kinckle Jones stated that the mission of *Opportunity* was to "lay bare Negro life as it is."

The Messenger. Edited by socialists Asa Phillip Randolph and Chandler Owen, the *Messenger* prided itself on being "a protest periodical." Its editors often had a very different perspective on how African-Americans should respond to the social and political problems they faced. When World War I began, the *Crisis* and *Opportunity* urged black people to enlist in the military. The *Messenger,* on the other hand, believed that black people should not fight for a country that promoted racial violence and discrimination. Randolph and Owen were arrested and jailed for their antigovernment response, and copies of the *Messenger* were confiscated and destroyed.

The Negro World. Edited by Marcus Garvey, who declared, "I started *The Negro World* to preserve the term Negro for the race as against the desperate desire of other newspapermen to substitute the term 'coloured' for the race." The *Negro World* was the official publication of the United Negro Improvement Association (UNIA). Published in English, Spanish, and French, it was distributed in the United States, Africa, and the Caribbean and boasted the largest circulation of any black paper during the Harlem Renaissance, with more than 200,000 readers.

The Liberator. Edited by Max Eastman, the *Liberator* often featured the powerful essays and poems of Claude McKay, one of the magazine's staff editors.

Fire!! The subtitle of the November 1926 issue read, "Devoted to Younger Negro Artists." Edited by Wallace Thurman, this one-time publication was the work of Harlem Renaissance writers and artists including Langston Hughes, Zora Neale Hurston, Arthur Fauset, Gwendolyn Bennett, Waring Cuney, Richard Nugent, and Aaron Douglas (who designed the dramatic red and black cover). *Fire!!* addressed issues that the Harlem elite did not care to see in print. The magazine failed after only one issue due to lack of support.

The New Masses. Discouraged by the ongoing problems of lynching and discrimination, some African-Americans began to explore the beliefs of other political parties. The *New Masses* was a journal that sought to recruit Harlemites to join the Communist Party.

Century Magazine. Edited by Carl Van Doren, *Century* published the pre-Renaissance poems of James Weldon Johnson, along with the works of numerous writers of the Harlem Renaissance. Carl Van Doren pledged "a genuine faith in the future of imaginative writing among Negroes in the United States."

The Nation. This magazine was a forum for the famous debate between Langston Hughes and George Schuyler, the *Nation's* editor. Schuyler believed that the Harlem Renaissance was a hoax, and that African people in America did not have a separate or special culture to celebrate. The *Nation* stirred a dialogue that continues even today.

Survey Graphic. A mainstream cultural magazine edited by Paul Kellogg. Fascinated by the creative genius of African-American writers and artists, Kellogg enlisted Alain Locke to edit a special issue of *Survey Graphic* devoted to the Harlem creative community. The issue, titled "Harlem: Mecca of the New Negro" was published in 1925 and sold out two printings.

New York Age. The oldest African-American newspaper in New York. For years, it featured the editorials of James Weldon Johnson, who worked as a staff editor there for ten years.

The Brownies' Book. A short-lived magazine of the NAACP, designed for black children. The *Brownies' Book* was edited by Jessie Redmon Fauset and W. E. B. Du Bois.

James Mercer Langston Hughes

Poet and Writer
1902–1967

James Mercer Langston Hughes was born in 1902, in Joplin, Missouri. Shortly after his birth his parents divorced and Langston's father went to live in Mexico. Langston was moved from city to city as his mother searched for work. When he was eight years old, he went to live with his grandmother. She told him stories about Sojourner Truth, shared the poetry of Paul Laurence Dunbar, and introduced him to the *Crisis* magazine, through which

he became acquainted with the writings of W. E. B. Du Bois. When Langston was twelve, his grandmother died and he went to live with family friends for two years. When his mother remarried, Langston rejoined his family in Lincoln, Illinois, and eventually moved to Cleveland, Ohio, where he attended Central High School.

After Hughes graduated from high school, he went to Mexico to visit his father. On his long journey, he traveled through the southern United States by train. As he crossed the Mississippi River, there was a beautiful sunset. This inspired him to write his famous poem "The Negro Speaks of Rivers," which he dedicated to W. E. B. Du Bois. He sent the poem to Jessie Redmon Fauset, literary editor of the *Crisis,* who published it in the magazine in 1921. Hughes spent fifteen months with his father, who promised to pay for his college education if he took up engineering. When he returned to the United States, he enrolled in Columbia University in New York. Although he earned good grades, with a B+ average, his heart was not in engineering. The following year he dropped out of Columbia, took a job as a steward on the SS *Malone,* and sailed for Africa. Hughes visited more than thirty ports including ones in Senegal, Nigeria, the Cameroons, Belgian Congo, Angola, and Guinea in Africa, then Italy, the Netherlands, Spain, and France. He continued to write poetry and submit it to the *Crisis.*

When he returned to the United States in 1924, the Harlem Renaissance and the Jazz Age were in full swing. First he moved to Harlem, then on to Washington, D.C., in 1925. Hughes loved the new African-American sound and began to frequent jazz nightspots, where he listened to music and wrote poetry. "I tried to write poems like the songs they sang on Seventh Street . . . [these songs] had the pulse beat of the people who keep on going," he said. Langston Hughes was the first writer to incorporate blues and jazz rhythms in his poetry. Some say his poems were written "to be read aloud, crooned, shouted, and sung."

In 1925, Hughes's poetry was included in Alain Locke's anthology, *The New Negro*. On May 25 of that same year, Hughes was among the prizewinners at *Opportunity* magazine's annual literary competition. That night, when James Weldon Johnson read Langston's poem "The Weary Blues," it sparked the interest of Carl Van Vechten, who encouraged Alfred A. Knopf to publish Hughes's first collection of poetry, also titled *The Weary Blues* (1926).

Hughes received a scholarship to Lincoln University in Pennsylvania, where he completed his undergraduate degree in 1929. No matter where he lived he always returned to Harlem regularly. In 1926, he wrote his most famous essay, "The Negro Artist and the Racial Mountain," in response to an essay written by the *Nation* editor George Schuyler. Schuyler did not believe that African-Americans had a distinct culture, separate and different from that of white Americans. Langston Hughes not only felt that black people had a unique culture, but that they should embrace and celebrate it in their art and music. Hughes frowned on African-American writers who took offense at being regarded as "Negro poets." He wrote, "No great poet has ever been afraid of being himself."

Hughes believed that the purest form of art came from the experience of the common man, his words and thoughts. But many of the Harlem elite had little appreciation for anything common. They could not see the value in celebrating their slave roots or their rural southern heritage. And they certainly did not care to make public the unique and private struggles of black folk. In November 1926, Wallace Thurman, Zora Neale Hurston, Hughes, and others published a new literary journal, *Fire!!* But the Harlem elite did not like its bold, revealing tone and refused to support the quarterly. Publication ended after the first issue.

Hughes met Charlotte Mason, the self-styled godmother of the Harlem Renaissance, while he was still a student at Lincoln University.

When she left him, she pressed a $50 bill into the palm of his hand and said, "A gift for a young poet." Mason became Hughes's patron, supporting him financially so that he could be free to write. That summer, instead of working the usual host of menial jobs, Hughes was free to complete his first novel, *Not without Laughter,* which was published in 1930. Throughout the 1930s, the prolific Hughes published poems, novels, and plays. In 1935, his play *The Mulatto* opened on Broadway. By this time, the Harlem Renaissance had ended. Hughes won a Guggenheim Fellowship and traveled to the Soviet Union, Haiti, Japan, and Spain. Like many African-Americans who were disappointed with their ongoing economic and social struggles, Hughes turned to communism.

In 1937 during the Spanish Civil War, he worked as a newspaper correspondent for the *Baltimore Afro-American.* In 1940, he penned an autobiography, *The Big Sea.* That same year he received the Rosenwald Fellowship. Langston Hughes wrote a total of sixteen books of poetry, two novels, three short story collections, four volumes of "editorial" and "documentary" fiction, twenty plays, children's poetry and nonfiction, musicals and operas, three autobiographies, a dozen radio and television scripts and dozens of magazine articles. In addition, he edited seven anthologies. No wonder he was considered the Poet Laureate of Harlem.

Hughes spent his later years writing, teaching, and mentoring other writers. He died of cancer in 1967. Since then, his home in Harlem has been designated a historical landmark, and the block where it is located was renamed Langston Hughes Place. The Langston Hughes Community Library and Cultural Center in Queens opened in 1969. It houses the largest circulating black heritage reading collection in New York City.

Countee Cullen

Poet
1903–1946

During the Harlem Renaissance, Alain Locke and Marcus Garvey urged African-Americans to celebrate Africa as a source of inspiration. This meant that the standard of beauty in life, literature, and art would be based on African-centered ideas rather than on white American or European definitions of beauty. Some African-Americans felt torn. Life in white America was the only life they knew, and they could not understand a need

or purpose in looking to Africa. In his poem "Heritage," Countee Cullen asked, "What is Africa to me?" Much like poet Jean Toomer, Cullen resented being defined by race. He told Langston Hughes he wanted to be a poet, not a Negro poet. He wanted to compete successfully on the white man's ground—and he did.

Countee Cullen was born Countee Porter in New York City on May 30, 1903. Not much is known about his real parents. As a young boy, a woman thought to be his maternal grandmother raised him. At fifteen, he went to live with Reverend and Mrs. Frederick Ashbury Cullen. Reverend Cullen was the pastor of Salem Methodist Episcopal Church, one of the largest congregations in Harlem at that time.

Countee began writing poetry in elementary school. He attended the finest schools and achieved recognition for his work as early as high school. His first published poem, "I Have a Rendezvous with Life," appeared in 1921, in the DeWitt Clinton High School literary magazine, the *Magpie,* which he later edited.

One of only a few African-Americans at DeWitt Clinton, Cullen excelled in all his studies, graduating with honors in Latin, mathematics, English, history, and French. In 1922, Cullen went to study at New York University (NYU), where his poetry was published in the literary magazines *Bookman* and *Poetry.* He also won the Witter Brynner Undergraduate Poetry Prize for "Ballad of the Brown Girl." Harvard University's Lyman Kittredge celebrated Cullen's poem as "the finest literary ballad by an American writer he had ever read."

The year 1925 was one of honors and achievements for Countee Cullen. Just before graduation, he received a contract with Harper to publish his first book of poems, *Color.* Not only did Cullen graduate from NYU with honors, but he was elected to the prestigious Phi Beta Kappa honor society and was accepted to Harvard University for graduate studies. In May 1925, he won second place in a competition sponsored by *Opportunity* magazine for his poem, "To One Who Said Me Nay." While attending Harvard, he became the assistant editor of *Opportunity.* He also contributed a regular column titled "The Dark Tower," after another of his poems.

Cullen believed that poetry should express beauty and truth, elements that cannot be confined to any one race. He felt that the reader should not be able to identify him as a black or white writer by his poems. Cullen sought to master the European classic poetry traditions. As a result, his writing style was very controlled. He rarely used harsh words or humor.

It often required more than pretty words and rhymes to depict Negro life in the 1920s. Lynchings and other race-related violence was all too common. But Cullen's conservative style didn't keep him from addressing racism and its impact. He often wrote about the difference between how whites and blacks were treated in America. In his poem "Yet Do I Marvel," he questioned why God would inspire him to write, yet make him black:

> *Yet do I marvel at this curious thing:*
> *To make a poet black and bid him sing*

It frustrated Cullen that black writers were not judged fairly on the strength of their writings.

In 1927, Cullen's second book of poetry, *Copper Sun,* was published, and he edited *Caroling Dust.* Cullen received the Harmon Foundation Literary Award and a Guggenheim Fellowship for study abroad. From 1928 to 1934, he traveled frequently between the United States and France. Many young African-American artists and writers such as William Johnson, Augusta Savage, Claude McKay, and Zora Neale Hurston visited France to study and perfect their craft.

Cullen was an important and well-known figure in the Harlem Renaissance and on the social scene. In fact, A'Lelia Walker Robinson Wilson, daughter of the black millionaire Madame C. J. Walker, opened a stylish tearoom and named it after Countee's poem "The Dark Tower." Just before his departure for France, he became engaged to Nina Yolande Du Bois, daughter of W. E. B. Du Bois. They married later that year, in a wedding described as the most important social event of the Harlem Renaissance. The marriage ended only a year later.

Cullen went on to publish more of his writings, including two children's books. From 1934 until his death in 1946, he taught English, French, and creative writing at the Frederick Douglass Junior High School. He worked with Arna Bontemps on *St. Louis Woman*, a play-turned-musical. Cullen died January 10, 1946, a few months before the play opened on Broadway. The *New York Times* headline read, "Countee Cullen, Negro Poet, Dead." Three thousand people attended the funeral.

The 135th Street branch of the New York Public Library, where Cullen was known to recite his poetry, was named in his honor. In recent years, a statue of Countee Cullen has also been erected.

Cullen's other verse collections include *Ballad of the Brown Girl* (1927) and *The Black Christ* (1929). His novel *One Way to Heaven* was published in 1931.

Claude McKay

Before Langston Hughes or Countee Cullen, there was Claude McKay. Claude McKay came to Harlem, New York, as a published writer. Born in 1890, in SunnyValle, Jamaica, Claude was introduced to poetry and English novels as a young boy by his brother, who had an extensive collection of books. In 1912, McKay published two collections of his poetry, *Songs of Jamaica* and *Constab Ballads.* He moved to the United States to study agriculture, attending Tuskegee Institute and Kansas State University.

To support himself, McKay worked aboard railroad dining cars, until he met a traveling black theater group. Members of the group suggested that New York was the place to be. By 1917, McKay had moved to New York where he mastered the sonnet form of writing poetry and published "The Harlem Dancer" and "Invocation." McKay's powerful use of the sonnet helped to inspire the Harlem Renaissance.

In 1919, race riots and assaults against blacks were rampant. Lynch mobs of angry whites went into black neighborhoods across America and launched violent attacks on blacks. Claude McKay's sonnet "If We Must Die" was published that year in the *Liberator.* This work was his passionate response to the murder and bloodshed of that period. He wrote:

> *O kinsmen we must meet the common foe!*
> *Though far outnumbered let us show us brave,*
> *And for their thousand blows deal one deathblow!*

"If We Must Die" made no mention of race. McKay wanted his sonnet to address not only the problems between blacks and whites in America, but to have universal meaning that crossed cultures and could apply to any group who had been "abused, outraged and murdered, whether they are minorities or nations, black or brown or yellow or white." Those who had assumed McKay was a white poet soon discovered he was of African descent. Suddenly, the powerful and defiant tone of the sonnet was perceived as a threat to white Americans. This was a disappointing development for McKay. Years later, he found satisfaction in news that a copy of the famous sonnet was discovered among the belongings of a white soldier who died on the Russian front in World War II. His universal message was felt after all.

For African-Americans, "If We Must Die" was hailed as a call for action and militancy. The message to blacks was to resist those who would oppress them and to take action. This was the driving spirit behind the New Negro movement.

McKay received financial support from a white Jamaican who urged him to use Jamaican dialect in his debut works. Over the years, he continued to use dialect in his poetry. By 1922, white patrons who supported what was called primitivism in the arts encouraged the work of writers such as McKay who used dialect in their writing.

After coming to New York, McKay was supported by another patron, Frank Harris, who was the editor of *Pearson's Magazine.* Later, he worked under Max Eastman at the *Liberator.* Their friendship spanned more than thirty years. Eastman provided invaluable assistance in publishing McKay's most popular works and later praised him, saying McKay "will live in history as the first great lyric genius that his race produced."

Although McKay's poems were regarded as "racially conscious" work, he rarely made mention of race in his writing until the 1922 release of his book *Harlem Shadows,* which included the poem "To My White Friend." In this piece, McKay warned, "Be not deceived, for every deed you do I could match—out-match: Am I not Africa's son." McKay became known for the bold, rebellious, and bitter tone of his poetry. Through his work, McKay reacted to the discrimination, oppression, and injustice in black life, putting into words the frustration and anger of many African-Americans. In contrast, McKay also wrote poems about romance and his love for nature.

McKay decided to travel to Europe to see how blacks were treated there. He also wanted to study communism, to see if this form of government was an answer to the race problem. He returned to America angry and dismayed, without a solution to racism in America. Still, McKay achieved a great deal during his journey abroad. He completed two books, *Home to*

Harlem and *Banjo: A Story without a Plot* (1928). These rich stories were the first of his published novels and turned out to be among his most celebrated works. *Home to Harlem* brought readers a view of Harlem from the common man's life experience—a view that some members of the black elite did not consider entertaining. In addition, the novel poked fun at the values of white society, the same values many middle-class African-Americans aspired to achieve. Despite some negative opinions of the book, *Home to Harlem* was the first novel by a Harlem writer to make the best-seller list.

McKay wrote other novels, including *Gingertown* (1932) and *Banana Bottom* (1933). His autobiography *A Long Way from Home* was published in 1937. McKay will always be remembered as the first poet to give voice to the New Negro. His work was enjoyed for more than forty years after the Harlem Renaissance ended. He died in 1948.

Jean Toomer

Writer and Poet
1894–1967

*A*fter several years' work, suddenly, it was as if a door opened and I knew without a doubt what I was "inside." I knew literature. And "what" was my joy!

It has been said that nothing in his appearance indicated that Jean Toomer was a black man. His straight hair, light olive complexion, and slender nose were a result of his mother's mixed heritage. Toomer disliked being labeled as Negro, and this troubled him throughout his career.

Named after both his father and grandfather, Jean Toomer was born Nathan Pinchback Toomer in Washington, D.C., on December 26, 1894. When his father left the family shortly after his birth, his mother renamed him Eugene. Toomer took the name of Jean in his early twenties around the same time that he became fascinated with the character called Jean Valjean in Victor Hugo's *Les Miserables* and with Romain Rolland's character Jean-Christophe.

Some might describe Jean as fickle because he changed his mind quite often. Less than four years after graduating from Dunbar High School, he had already attended five colleges. He studied agriculture at the University of Wisconsin. Six months later he moved to Massachusetts to attend the Massachusetts College of Agriculture, but just before enrolling, he had a change of heart and briefly pursued his interest in physical fitness at the American College of Physical Training in Chicago. Toomer's willingness to follow his heart, however, also led him to a career in writing and to make such a memorable contribution to the literature of the Harlem Renaissance.

While studying physical fitness, Toomer decided to take additional classes at the University of Chicago, where he first discovered his love for reading. Toomer read books on philosophy, religion, and psychology. He also read literary magazines and novels such as *Moby Dick* by Herman Melville and poetry such as *Inferno* in Dante's *Divine Comedy*. This reading inspired Toomer to write his first story, "Bona and Paul."

With a strong thirst for knowledge, the young writer took every opportunity to learn more about the subjects that peaked his curiosity. In 1917, after reading *Dynamic Sociology*, Toomer moved to New York and took two courses in sociology at New York University. "Never in my life had I read such a book. I felt I must return to college where I could get an ordered study on the subject," Toomer stated. He also enrolled in history classes at the City University of New York. It was during this time in New York that Jean Toomer read a book by Johann Goethe, *Wilhelm Meister*, which changed his life. Toomer described the experience: "It seemed to gather all the scattered parts of myself. . . . And for the first time in years I breathed the air of my own land. . . . I resolved to devote myself to making myself such a person as I caught glimpses of in the pages of *Wilhelm Meister*. For my specialized work, I would write."

By 1920, Toomer had settled in Manhattan and was introduced to the New York literary scene. But soon, he had to return to Washington, D.C., to care for his ailing grandfather. Toomer's time in Washington was a blessing in disguise. He was able to produce several manuscripts. Exhausted from writing and his responsibilities with his grandfather, Toomer decided to take a break and accepted a job as school principal in Sparta, Georgia. Toomer had never lived in the Deep South and was so moved by the experience that he believed he had discovered his ancestral roots in Sparta. In fact, he was so inspired that he created stories and characters to share his rich cultural experience.

Jean Toomer returned to Washington in December 1921. Shortly after his grandfather died, he completed the first draft of *Cane*, a collection of prose poetry in which Jean combined his Sparta-inspired works with writings from his time in Washington and Chicago. This combination offered readers an opportunity to examine and contrast the traditions and culture of the Deep South with the attitudes and values of the New Negro of the North.

Toomer began to send his favorite poetry and prose selections from *Cane* to New York book and magazine publishers. He also sent several pieces to famed author and close friend Waldo Frank at his request. Writers of the Harlem Renaissance supported and promoted the work of other

The Gurdjieff Group

writers they admired. Alain Locke published Toomer's "Song of Son" in the *Crisis,* the official publication of the National Association for the Advancement of Colored People (NAACP). Claude McKay published "Becky," "Reapers," and "Carma" in the *Liberator.* Toomer's work was so well received that eleven pieces from the *Cane* collection were published in 1922. During the Harlem Renaissance, the book had only two small printings in 1923 and 1927, but it gave readers meaningful and powerful images of Sparta,

Georgia. As a result, this small, southern town was later referenced in the writings of Zora Neale Hurston and Langston Hughes, who traveled there in the summer of 1927.

Jean Toomer was proud of his achievement with *Cane*, but the book's foreword written by Waldo Frank left him frustrated and troubled and marked the beginning of the end of their friendship. First, Frank used the term "Negro" in his foreword and clearly identified Toomer as African-American. Because of his appearance, Toomer was rarely asked about his race. It was not his intention to deny his race. But during this era, whites most often regarded outstanding achievements by African-Americans as contributions to their race that could only be measured within the boundaries of the black community. Toomer wanted to be recognized as a human being and as an American first. He resented being classified as a great African-American writer. He would have preferred to be known as a great American writer. In his poem "People," he shared his views on race:

> *O people, if you but used*
> *Your other eyes*
> *You would see beings.*

Toomer's study of religion and psychology led him to Fontainebleau, France, to study Unitism, a religion found by the Armenian George Ivanovitch Gurdjieff. He returned to New York and opened the Gurdjieff Group in Harlem, in 1925, attracting others from the Renaissance community including Langston Hughes, Zora Neale Hurston, Wallace Thurman, Nella Larsen, Harold Jackman, Dorothy Peterson, and artist Aaron Douglas. Inspired by this new way of thinking, Langston Hughes wrote a piece titled "Gurdjieff in Harlem," in his book *The Big Sea*.

Toomer later joined the Quaker Society of Friends, but then returned to studies with Gurdjieff. He produced a body of work related to his spiritual and philosophical thoughts and continued to write poetry and prose as well.

Toomer died at his New York home in 1967. Two years later, in 1969, *Cane* was reprinted and hailed as an early motivating work of the Harlem Renaissance and today is still recognized as an African-American literary classic.

Arnaud "Arna" Bontemps

Writer and Educator
1902–1973

*Let us keep the dance of
rain our fathers kept
And tread our dreams
beneath the jungle sky.*

Arna Bontemps was fifteen years old when his father sent him to the all-white San Fernando Boarding Academy with one instruction—not to "act colored" there. In an autobiographical essay, Arna later challenged, "How dare anyone, parent, schoolteacher, or merely literary critic, tell me not to act colored. . . . Why should I be ashamed of such influence?" As an adult, Arna not only learned to embrace those behaviors that others considered "acting colored," he committed his life's work to the preservation of African-American folklore and culture.

Arnaud Wendell Bontemps was born in 1902 in Alexandria, Louisiana. This small southern town was a difficult place for the Bontemps to live. With the gold rush of the 1890s, California was still considered "the new frontier," a land of opportunity. So after a series of "racial incidents," Paul and Maria Bontemps decided to move their family out west, first to San Francisco, then on to Los Angeles. Arna grew up in a neighborhood still known today as Watts.

Arna's mother died in 1914, when he was twelve years old. That same year, he began working as a newsboy and gardener to help his family. After completing boarding school, he attended Pacific Union College (now UCLA) where he first developed an interest in writing. He completed his bachelor's degree in only three short years and graduated in 1923, just when the Harlem Renaissance was gaining momentum. By 1924, he had a poem published in the *Crisis* magazine and a job offer to teach at Harlem Academy in New York. Bontemps thrived on the energy of Harlem. He wrote, "In some places the autumn of 1924 may have been an unremarkable season. In Harlem it was like a foretaste of paradise." Bontemps's poetry was award winning. He won *Opportunity* magazine's Alexander Pushkin Poetry Award in 1926 and 1927. He also won the *Crisis* poetry contest in 1927.

Bontemps was a talented essayist, children's writer, and novelist. His writing was a tribute to African-American culture, often honoring the spirituals, blues, and jazz. Bontemps believed it was important to record history and to write books for children. In 1931, he published his first children's book, *God Sends Sunday*. This was followed by *You Can't Pet a Possum*

(1934), and *Sad-Faced Boy* (1937). In 1956, his book *Story of the Negro* was named a Newbery Honor Book by the American Library Association.

After the Harlem Renaissance was over, Bontemps published numerous accounts that documented the people, the life, and the literature of the era. He wrote the biography of the Father of the Blues, W. C. Handy, and edited *The Book of Negro Folklore, American Negro Poetry,* and *100 Years of Negro Freedom.* A great friend of writer Langston Hughes, Bontemps worked with Hughes on several anthologies. He also cowrote a play with Countee Cullen. Bontemps won two Rosenwald Fellowships, in 1928 and 1942, and two Guggenheim Fellowships, in 1948 and 1954.

Bontemps who had trained in library science took a position as head librarian at Fisk University in Nashville, Tennessee. He brought his fierce dedication to preserving African-American culture to his new position. Bontemps did his best to ensure that the art and literature of the Harlem Renaissance would be preserved for future generations. While at Fisk, he started the Langston Hughes Renaissance Collection, which included the writings of Hughes, James Weldon Johnson, Countee Cullen, Jean Toomer, and Charles Johnson. He knew so many writers and artists from his days in Harlem that he was able to call upon others such as W. C. Handy and Carl Van Vechten, who donated his music collection. After more than twenty years at Fisk, Bontemps retired but he was not through teaching or writing. He became a professor at the University of Illinois in Chicago in 1966. It was there that he wrote *The Great Slave Narratives.*

Three years later he was asked to lecture and serve as curator of the James Weldon Johnson Memorial Collection of Negro Arts and Letters at Yale University, in New Haven, Connecticut. By 1971, Bontemps had returned to Fisk University as a writer in residence. The next year, he published his autobiography *The Harlem Renaissance Remembered.* Bontemps died of a heart attack in 1973.

Nella Larsen

Writer
1891–1964

In the early 1900s, being black was viewed as a curse by some African-Americans. Though slavery had ended, life was very hard for black people in America. In much of America, black people lived in constant fear of racial hatred and violence. Some blacks wished they could simply shed their skin and live free from discrimination. And some of them did exactly that.

Passing for white was not uncommon among blacks and mulattoes who had fair skin and European features. Nella Larsen was a mulatto—her mother was a white Danish immigrant and her father was a black man from the Virgin Islands. She was born Nella Walker in 1891. It was reported that Nella's mother had divorced her father, Peter Walker, and married a white man, Peter Larsen. But historians now believe that Peter Walker and Peter Larsen were the same man and that Nella's father changed his name to Larsen when he began passing for white.

Nella was the odd child of the family. Although she had light skin, she was the only family member who could not pass for white. In 1907, Peter Larsen enrolled Nella in Fisk University Normal School. At that time, Fisk was both a high school and a university. After Nella started school, her family decided to continue passing for white, and they cut all ties with their daughter.

Completely without a family, Larsen moved to New York to study nursing in 1912. By 1915, she had graduated and accepted a position as head nurse at Tuskegee Institute's John Andrew Memorial Hospital and Nurse Training School. A year later, she moved back to New York and continued nursing. In 1919, she married physicist Elmer Imes, who became the chairman of the physics department at Fisk. Historically black universities such as Fisk and Howard played an important role in supporting the writers and artists of the Harlem Renaissance, providing both educational resources and opportunities for creative young people to showcase their talent. As a result, Larsen became an active part of Harlem's social scene before her writing was widely recognized.

While still working as a nurse, Nella wrote a couple of articles on Danish games for the *Brownies' Book,* the NAACP children's magazine edited by famed Harlem Renaissance writer Jessie Redmon Fauset. In 1921, Larsen quit her nursing job and took a position at the 135th Street branch of the New York Public Library. The library was an important place for

Harlem Renaissance writers, and Nella was becoming part of that community. There writers and artists exhibited their works. Larsen also returned to school to study library science at Columbia University.

Larsen's work as a writer is filled with disappearing acts because she often published under imaginary names. One of her only known pen names was Allen Semi, a combination of her first name and her married name, spelled backward. By 1928, Larsen finally gathered the courage to publish her first novel under her own name. *Quicksand* established Larsen's voice as an important part of the literary dialogue of the Harlem Renaissance. Larsen received a bronze medal from the Harmon Foundation for her outstanding book that explored the mulatto's dilemma of living in two worlds. W. E. B. Du Bois praised her novel as "the best piece of fiction that Negro America has produced since the heyday of Chesnutt" (referring to early African-American writer Charles W. Chesnutt, who also wrote of the mulatto experience).

Larsen's second novel, *Passing,* was not as well received. *Passing* was a novel about two black women, one of whom passes for white and marries a man who hates African-Americans. Though the characters were fictional, Larsen's painful personal experience and her feelings about her family's secret lives had a lot to do with her decision to write about this subject.

Not long after the release of *Passing,* Larsen published the story "Sanctuary" in *Forum Magazine* in January 1930 and was accused of plagiarism. The charges were denied by Larsen and her supporters, but they haunted her, as did problems in her marriage, which ended in 1933. From that point on, her work remained unpublished. Larsen virtually disappeared. She moved out of Harlem and told friends that she was going to South America, when in fact she remained in New York. Just as her family had severed ties, Larsen cut herself off from her Harlem friends. She later returned to the nursing profession. It is a mystery whether or not Larsen continued to write and publish her stories. Nella Larsen died on March 30, 1964.

Zora Neale Hurston

Writer and Anthropologist
1901–1960

I am not tragically colored. There is no great sorrow dammed up in my soul, nor lurking behind my eyes. . . . No I do not weep at the world—I am too busy sharpening my oyster knife.

These are the proud words of Zora Neale Hurston. Zora's childhood was very different from that of most African-Americans. Zora was born in Notasulga, Alabama, but she grew up in the first incorporated all-black town in the United

States, Eatonville, Florida, where her father was mayor and a Baptist preacher. Her family moved to this all-black town shortly afterward.

Tragedy struck the Hurston family when Zora was nine—her mother died. By the age of fourteen, Zora was supporting herself with jobs as a maid and as a wardrobe assistant to a touring theatrical company. After her father remarried, she left home and went to Baltimore, where she enrolled in night school. Several months later, she moved to Washington, D.C., where, in 1918, she attended Howard University and became involved in writing. In 1925, Zora won a scholarship and became the first African-American student to earn a bachelor's degree from Barnard College in New York.

That year, *Opportunity* magazine hosted a dinner at the Civic Club where they held their first annual literary contest. Hurston won several awards. Her essays and short stories were published in *Opportunity,* the *Crisis,* and other publications. She became editor of the *Spokesman* and changed the journal's focus to black folklore.

In 1926, Hurston and a group of young artists and writers, including Langston Hughes, Wallace Thurman, and Aaron Douglas decided to publish a literary magazine to their own liking—*Fire!!* This new magazine challenged the conservative tastes of the Harlem elite. The magazine failed after only one issue, however, because of lack of support.

It was hard to make a living as a writer. Hurston supported herself by waitressing or working as a maid. She met famed anthropologist Franz Boas and decided to take a graduate degree in anthropology to study black folk cultures. But scrubbing floors and waiting tables could not pay her living expenses at Columbia, and Hurston knew she needed a wealthy patron. Many artists of the Renaissance had their incomes supplemented by wealthy patrons. Alain Locke had introduced Hurston to Charlotte Mason, better known as "the godmother." Mason insisted she be called by this endearing name because she didn't want anyone to know of her patronage.

She believed the black writers' goal should be to express their "primitive" or savage nature. She was known for making outrageous comments and demands in an effort to control the kind of work they produced.

Mason and her husband believed that African-Americans and Native Americans were the "child races" and that the "primitive" nature of these people had to be preserved. She insisted her artists and writers create works that fit this ideal. Unfortunately, her idea of primitive work represented a limited view of black culture that centered on racial stereotypes.

"Play fool to catch wise" is an African-American proverb that some might use to describe how Hurston survived in New York during the Harlem Renaissance. The godmother sponsored Hurston along with Louise Thompson and Langston Hughes. Though they all describe her as beautiful and generous, Louise Thompson said of the godmother, "Her black guests were primitive savages or they were not being themselves." Thompson and Hughes recalled that Hurston seemed comfortable with the arrangement, as if she were playing a game. Hurston tolerated the godmother until she made demands of Hurston's work that she was not willing to meet. Hurston refused to be defined by anyone. She wanted to be in full control of what she wrote. So, she and the godmother parted ways in 1932.

Hurston loved to write about real people. Her professor Franz Boas had encouraged her to travel and to document black life and culture. Hurston was awarded a Guggenheim Fellowship and traveled to Jamaica, Haiti, Bermuda, Honduras, and the southern United States conducting research. She even collected African-American folk songs so that she could share "real" black music in her writings. Her 1935 novel *Mules and Men* showcased the songs and the black folklore she'd discovered during her research in the South. In 1934, she published *Jonah's Gourd Vine*. It has been called the last novel of the Harlem Renaissance. *Jonah's Gourd Vine* and her

1937 release, *Their Eyes Were Watching God,* both take place in her hometown of Eatonville. The 1937 book received good reviews but few sales. In 1938, Hurston went to work for the Works Progress Administration (WPA) and continued her anthropological research. She continued to write and lecture and penned her autobiography, *Dust Tracks on a Road* (1942), but still could not earn enough money to support herself. In her later years, she worked in Florida as a maid.

Zora Neale Hurston died penniless of heart disease in Fort Pierce, Florida, on January 28, 1960, and was buried in an unmarked grave. Pulitzer Prize–winning author Alice Walker rediscovered the writings of Zora Neale Hurston. Since then, Hurston's work has been republished and appreciated by a new generation. Walker also found Hurston's unmarked grave and placed a headstone that reads, ZORA NEALE HURSTON; A GENIUS OF THE SOUTH; 1901–1960, NOVELIST, FOLKLORIST, ANTHROPOLOGIST.

Wallace Thurman

Writer and Editor
1902–1934

Wallace Thurman was one of the great thinkers of the Harlem Renaissance. Langston Hughes described him in his autobiography *The Big Sea* as "a strangely brilliant man who had read everything and whose critical mind could find something wrong with everything he read."

Wallace Thurman had come a long way to get to Harlem. Born in Salt Lake City, Utah, in 1902, Wallace went on to attend the University of Southern California. Like many writers of the New Negro movement, Thurman was drawn to the creative energy for which Harlem, New York, was rapidly becoming famous. He moved there in 1925 and immediately went to work for one of the three top black magazines in Harlem, the *Messenger*. Though his work as editor at the *Messenger* was short-lived, he made sure that the writings of Langston Hughes and Zora Neale Hurston were part of the magazine's regular content.

Thurman often challenged the ideas of leader W. E. B. Du Bois. He believed that the writings of the Harlem Renaissance should tell it like it is—and show both the good and the bad in black people. This was a controversial idea in the 1920s, and still is today—as critics of rap and hip-hop believe the music glorifies a view of black life that should not be celebrated. The goal of the New Negro movement was to show white America that blacks were not inferior, and many black leaders of that era believed that exposing certain aspects of Negro life would not help to achieve this end. Thurman disagreed.

Like many other writers and artists, Thurman lived rent-free in a boardinghouse at 267 West 136th Street, often referred to as "267 House," where his inner circle of friends would often join him for discussions and debates. Determined to carry out his ideas, Thurman asked his friends to join him in creating a new black literary magazine, *Fire!!* It didn't take much effort to convince this group. As Langston Hughes said, "We younger Negro artists who create now intend to express our dark selves without fear or shame." Zora Neale Hurston was 100 percent committed to *Fire!!* too. In her opinion, "*The Crisis* is the house organ of the NAACP and *Opportunity* is the same to the Urban League. They are in literature on the side."

Thurman agreed with Hurston. He had long criticized the quality of the existing magazines. He was determined to present a true literary magazine "worthy of the drawings of Aaron Douglas." Langston Hughes recalls, "It had to be what we seven young Negroes dreamed our magazine would be, in the end it cost almost a thousand dollars, and nobody could pay the bills." This was the first sign of trouble. Despite their lack of finances, Thurman convinced the printers to release the magazine with an IOU. The second sign of trouble was the cold reception *Fire!!* received from the Harlem elite. W. E. B. Du Bois was deeply hurt by the efforts of these writers whose essays and poetry had graced the pages of the *Crisis. Fire!!* received mixed reviews and was finished almost as soon as it began. It ended after the first issue. To make matters worse, the unsold issues of the failed literary magazine were lost when a fire burned down the house where they were stored.

Even four years later, every penny that Thurman earned went to pay the bills for the magazine's expensive production. Fortunately, Thurman's career as a writer did not end with *Fire!!* He was a hardworking man who was good at all sorts of writing. Thurman was the ghostwriter for the book *True Story* and secretly wrote the books of a number of well-known white writers. He was also the only black reader for Macaulay's, a large publisher. In 1928, he edited the book *Negro Life in New York's Harlem.* The following year, he published his first novel, *The Blacker the Berry: A Novel of Negro Life.* In the usual style of Wallace Thurman, his first novel addressed a topic that many African-Americans did not appreciate—the issue of skin color and prejudice against dark-skinned blacks within the black community. This book offended some and intrigued others. But regardless of their like or dislike for the book, they could not stop reading it.

That same year, a play written by Thurman and William Rapp called *Harlem* opened on Broadway. It received both positive and negative reviews, with the most negative reviews coming from the black critics. Still, Thurman was his own worst critic. He doubted his writing talent, was often depressed, and drank heavily. His last novel, *Infants of the Spring* (1932), marked the end of an era. The story poked fun at the cast of characters of the Harlem Renaissance in a playful way. But at the same time the story revealed Thurman's low self-esteem and his own bad feelings about his dark skin.

In 1932, he also published a novel he cowrote with Abraham Furman titled *The Interne*. By 1934, Thurman had expanded the scope of his writing to Hollywood. His final works were two screenplays, *Tomorrow's Children* (1935) and *High School Girl* (1935), the year he died. His death stunned friends. The Harlem community had just mourned the loss of writer Rudolph Fisher. Less than a week later, Thurman died in a charity hospital. Some say his heavy drinking killed him. Other reports say he died of tuberculosis.

Jessie Redmon Fauset

Writer
1882–1961

essie Redmon Fauset influenced just about every major writer of the Harlem Renaissance. Her apartment on 142nd Street was often filled with the laughter and conversation of the intellectuals and "niggerati" of the New Negro movement. Wallace Thurman and Zora Neale Hurston coined the term "niggerrati" to poke fun at the African-American political and social elite. They also used this term, with humor, to refer to themselves—the artists and writers of the Harlem Renaissance.

Jessie was born in 1882, in Fredericksville, New Jersey. Her father, Reverend Redmon Fauset, was pastor of an African Methodist Episcopal (AME) church in the nearby all-black community of Snow Hill. Snow Hill was part of the Underground Railroad system and was founded by Quakers who helped African-Americans escape from slavery. Jessie grew up in dramatically different surroundings in Philadelphia, Pennsylvania. The family moved there when she was still a baby. Though Jessie's parents were well-to-do, she experienced great hardship as a young girl, with the death of her mother and four of her seven brothers and sisters.

Fauset seemed to achieve despite these tragedies. She was the only black student at the Philadelphia High School for Girls where she was an A student. From there, she attended Cornell University. It is believed that she was the first African-American woman to graduate from that prestigious university. During her studies at Cornell, she met W. E. B. Du Bois, who offered her a summer job teaching at Fisk University. While at Cornell, Fauset was inducted into the Phi Beta Kappa honor society. After graduating from Cornell, Fauset tried to get a teaching position in her hometown of Philadelphia, but failed. Her first teaching job was in Baltimore, and then in 1906 she worked in Washington, D.C., at M Street High School. At that time M Street was considered one of the best schools for African-Americans in the United States. While in Washington, she began to work with the National Association for the Advancement of Colored People (NAACP). By 1912, her essays were already appearing in the *Crisis* magazine. Before settling in New York, Fauset traveled to the prestigious University of Paris and completed a master's degree in French from the University of Pennsylvania.

At the urging of her mentor, W. E. B. Du Bois, Fauset moved to Harlem in 1919 and took the job of literary editor for the *Crisis,* the official publication of the NAACP. It was one of the top black literary publications of the Harlem Renaissance and featured the poems, opinions, and stories of the top writers of the time. She also worked as editor for the *Brownies' Book*, the organization's children's magazine, which only lasted from 1920 to 1921. Writers who did not feel comfortable with Du Bois would approach Fauset with their work. She encouraged and published the writing of Langston Hughes, Jean Toomer, Arna Bontemps, Nella Larsen, Countee Cullen, and others.

Fauset spoke fluent French, and she used this knowledge to extend the readership of the *Crisis* abroad. She wrote book reviews and translations to help African-Americans become familiar with African and Caribbean writers whose works were written in French. In addition to being a multitalented editor, Jessie was a journalist. She traveled to London, Brussels, and Paris to cover the Second Pan-African Conference. She also wrote extensively in the *Crisis* about her experience at the 1922 meeting of the National Association of Colored Women, and about the mission of Mary McCleod Bethune and Haille Quinn Brown.

Fauset's first novel, *There Is Confusion,* was published in 1924. Charles S. Johnson, the editor of *Opportunity,* organized a dinner at the famed Civic Club in her honor. The gala event included all the major figures of the Harlem Renaissance including James Weldon Johnson, Langston Hughes, and Du Bois. In 1926, Fauset had a disagreement with Harlem Renaissance leader Alain Locke. That same year, she took a six-month journey to Africa. When she returned, she resigned as editor of the *Crisis,* and returned to teaching.

In 1927, Fauset joined the faculty of the prestigious Dewitt Clinton High School, the school that writer Countee Cullen and other Renaissance writers had attended. Leaving the *Crisis* did not affect her contribution to Harlem Renaissance literature. The following year, she published her second novel, *Plum Bun: A Novel without a Moral.* Most literary critics consider this her best book. *Plum Bun* is the story of a light-skinned black woman who decides to pass for white in New York City. All of Fauset's books take a look into the internal struggles of light-skinned African-Americans and mulattoes. In 1931, she published *The Chinaberry Tree: A Novel of American Life,* a book that dealt with the complicated issues that arise for people with one white and one black parent. *Comedy: American Style,* her fourth novel, published in 1933, was the story of a woman who ruined her family with her favoritism for her light-skinned children. Each of Fauset's four novels featured characters who were considered "upper class." This was a problem for critics who believed that her vision of African-Americans was too limited and ignored the contributions of the hardworking lower class.

Though Fauset's novels received mixed reviews, her upper-class characters were a very real part of the African-American community, and their painful stories earned her a special place in Harlem Renaissance literature. Jessie Redmon Fauset not only created literature, but she encouraged and mentored the best writers as an editor and educator, making her contribution truly extraordinary.

Sterling Allen Brown

Writer and Poet
1901–1989

Contrary to what the name suggests, the Harlem Renaissance was not confined to Harlem. Its impact was felt during the 1920s and 1930s in other black cities. Artists, writers, political activists, and educators of African descent from as near as Atlanta, Georgia, and as far away as Africa's Ivory Coast became a part of the exciting dialogues this movement generated. Sterling Brown spent a great deal of the Harlem Renaissance in Washington, D.C., where he had been born in 1901; he was part of the faculty of Howard University for almost sixty years.

In 1925, he had graduated from Williams College, having been inducted into the Phi Beta Kappa honor society. Shortly afterward, Brown attended the famous dinner that honored winners of *Opportunity* magazine's first annual literary awards. He sat and celebrated among the other prizewinners whose names read like a who's who of young Harlem Renaissance writers— Langston Hughes, Countee Cullen, Zora Neale Hurston, Eric Walrond, E. Franklin Frasier, and Frank Horne. From there, Brown attended Harvard University, where he earned a master's degree in 1930. Brown was an educator, teaching at a number of universities and colleges including Virginia Seminary in Lynchburg, Virginia; Fisk University in Nashville, Tennessee; Lincoln University in Jefferson City, Missouri; Vassar College in New York City; Atlanta University; and New York University. Historically black universities were a vital part of the Harlem Renaissance. They were among the few places that black artists could exhibit their work. They also provided a nurturing community for black intellectuals and writers.

In 1929, Brown returned to Howard University, where he was a professor of English, and maintained his university affiliation almost until his death in 1989. His students include such notables as Ossie Davis, Amiri Baraka, Gwendolyn Brooks, Stokely Carmichael, and Nobel laureate Toni Morrison.

A poet, literary critic, and educator, Brown's messages rang loud and clear during the New Negro movement. He is credited with being a founder of black literary criticism. There is no doubt that he was downright honest in his opinions about current books, essays, and plays. For the first time in history, African-Americans were deciding what books were important and why, rather than being told by others. Brown believed that white writers did not do a good job of creating realistic black characters in their books. He felt that too often their black characters' lives and reactions were based on racist stereotypes of what they believed it was like to be black. He felt that black writers were the most qualified to relate the most truthful, accurate accounts of black life. Brown became fascinated with black folk culture of the South. He dedicated his life to honoring the spiritual songs that came about during slavery and the many ways in which the African heritage was expressed in the way black people walked and talked. He wanted to bring the true "Negro experience" to the world through poetry and novels that could be enjoyed by the world. He wanted to show African-Americans that their southern roots were a part of their history they could appreciate, rather than hide in shame.

Using southern dialect and genuine examples of folk music and song, his first published collection of poetry thrust his work into the company of writers such as Jean Toomer, Claude McKay, Countee Cullen, and Langston Hughes. This particular style of writing was called black folk literature and focused on the triumphs of the common man over adversity and society's efforts to change him. The words and thoughts his characters spoke were thought to be so genuine that his work was beyond criticism.

His first novel, *Southern Road,* used the exact language of working-class people of the rural South. Brown could not find a publisher for his second book and did not publish again until 1975. He has been described as the most underrated poet of the Harlem Renaissance. But Brown continued to write and to publish and by 1979, his writings had regained public interest. In 1979, May 1 was declared "Sterling A. Brown Day" in Washington, D.C. Sterling bragged in a *Washington Post* interview, "I have been rediscovered, reinstituted, regenerated, and recovered," In 1980, he won the Lenore Marshall Prize for "best book of poetry" for his *Collected Poems of Sterling Brown.* In 1984, he was named poet laureate of the District of Columbia.

Carl Van Vechten

Writer and Photographer
1880–1964

The historian Nathan Huggins once said that Carl Van Vechten was a collector of rare objects and of rare people. "He enjoyed the discovery, and he enjoyed the display," Huggins said. Carl was white, but he practically made a career out of promoting African-American artists, both socially and professionally. He used his fame and influence to help African-American writers, artists, and performers gain the recognition they deserved. His pioneering efforts opened the doors of opportunity for some of the brightest talents of the Harlem Renaissance.

Carl was born in Cedar Rapids, Iowa, on June 17, 1880. Cedar Rapids was a prosperous town. In it, one could find a mix of industry, farm products, and the railroad—a steady passage of people and products, to and from the western frontier.

Carl's parents believed in treating all people with respect. They insisted on calling the African-American servants that they employed "Mr." and "Mrs." It may seem like a small thing, but for that time it was a meaningful daily gesture of dignity and respect.

Van Vechten left Iowa in 1899 for the University of Chicago. Chicago was a big, modern city with more opportunities for Van Vechten to study art, music, and opera. People at that time believed that the arts—painting, sculpture, music, and literature—had enduring value. The arts were thought to be the true evidence of all people's contribution to world civilization. Van Vechten loved to study different cultures. He was thrilled by the ways that different cultures expressed themselves in the arts—and he was willing to travel to learn more.

After graduating in 1903, Van Vechten worked at the *Chicago American* newspaper. In 1906, he moved to New York City and was hired as the assistant music critic for the *New York Times*.

If Chicago seemed exciting after Cedar Rapids, New York City was even more thrilling. Artists, musicians, writers, and singers were all trying to express what it meant to be American in their works. So far though, the only truly American forms of expression were spirituals and jazz—both products of African-Americans. Literature and the visual arts, for the most part, were imitating European traditions.

Starting in 1907, Van Vechten's interest in arts and culture led him to tour Europe. He returned to America and his job at the *New York Times* in

1909 and became the nation's first critic of a new art form known as modern dance. Modern dance was a bold break from classical ballet tradition. Rather than the stiff, formal postures of ballet, modern dance movements stressed the expression of inner feelings and emotion.

After publishing his first novel, *Peter Whiffle: His Life and Works* (1922), Van Vechten met Walter White, the black author and assistant secretary of the NAACP. Walter White showed Van Vechten all over Harlem. He introduced Van Vechten to important people at chic parties, lunches, and fancy dinners. After two weeks of that, Van Vechten said, "I knew every educated person in Harlem. I knew them by the hundreds."

Van Vechten recalled, "I frequented nightclubs a great deal. They were very popular at the time in New York. . . . I used to get other people to go and it became quite a rage . . . to go to night clubs in Harlem."

In the New York of those days, wealthy whites lived downtown, while Harlem was located uptown. Van Vechten became *the* downtown expert on Harlem nightlife. He was often asked to serve as a guide to the "authentic" places and the best entertainment for his wealthy downtown friends and visiting Europeans. "That was almost my fate, for ten years at least—taking people to Harlem," Van Vechten said.

Harlem was exciting to whites. Many thought that in Harlem's socials, nightclubs, and rent parties, they could find what they felt was missing in their own lives. The very air of Harlem seemed to be filled with energy, opportunity, and hope, not to mention the sweet sounds of jazz.

Part of the reason that Harlem was so popular was the widespread belief that white culture had lost its vitality, so whites looked to other cultures for ways to revive it. African art was inspiring whole new art forms and shaking up the painting and sculpture traditions of England, France, and Germany. African-American music was winning critical acclaim all over Europe, along with singers, dancers, and performers.

Many white writers and intellectuals believed that the so-called primitive races (meaning African, Asian, and Native American) led simpler, happier lives, free of the rules and stress that whites placed on themselves. They wrote articles, stories, and novels about what they imagined were the good primitive traits.

When white Americans and Europeans felt they needed some of the "innocence" and "childlike joy" of the Negro, they looked for it in Harlem. Van Vechten became known as the man who always knew where to find it.

But Van Vechten was not satisfied with hanging out uptown. So he did something completely unheard of. He invited his black friends from Harlem to his home downtown and to his infamous parties.

It was one thing to venture into the dark, smoky clubs of Harlem, but to actually invite blacks into white neighborhoods and white homes was shocking in 1923. It was so outrageous that it became chic, and other wealthy whites copied the idea.

This helped to spread the knowledge and interest in what African-American writers, actors, artists, and educators were working on. It also put talented African-Americans in direct contact with the people who could best help their careers. It was Carl Van Vechten who convinced his publisher, Alfred Knopf, to publish Langston Hughes's first book of poetry, *The Weary Blues,* in 1925. Hughes would go on to publish many books with Alfred Knopf's firm. With Van Vechten's help, James Weldon Johnson, Nella Larsen, Rudolph Fisher, and Chester Himes also earned publishing deals with Knopf.

Van Vechten's reputation as an important art critic grew as well, and Van Vechten was only too happy to use his influence and his pen to publicize African-American culture. Van Vechten used his contacts to convince the upper-class magazine *Vanity Fair* to include the works of many black writers. He also wrote numerous critical reviews of music, drama, literature, and art. Van Vechten explained, "Everything I wrote about Negroes was published, and this did a lot towards establishing them with other editors because at that time it was very rare to have a story about a Negro even in the newspapers. And the magazines!"

Then Van Vechten went beyond the parties and articles. He wrote a fictional novel about Harlem. Van Vechten's novel was the first truly popular book to portray African-Americans as individual people rather than as a negative stereotype. Van Vechten's book sold nearly 100,000 copies when it was first released in 1926. The title Van Vechten chose for his book, though, made many people doubt if he really was a friend to black Americans. He called his book *Nigger Heaven,* a term used to refer to the "blacks only" balcony section in theaters of the day.

Van Vechten insisted that he meant the title ironically. Irony is a way of showing that words can have two different meanings. He did not intend the word "nigger" to have a negative meaning. On the contrary, he worked hard to show that Harlem was a place of culture that drew the brightest blacks from everywhere. Still, there were those who said that Van Vechten chose the title just to startle people and create a sensation.

W. E. B. Du Bois did not like Van Vechten's book at all. He wrote at length on what he felt was wrong with it. Du Bois said that the title means, "a nasty, sordid corner where black people are herded, and yet a place which they in their crass ignorance are fools enough to enjoy. Harlem is no such place as that, and no one knows this better than Carl Van Vechten."

While Van Vechten's book was unique in the way he described life in Harlem, he was not alone in being a white man writing about African-Americans. With plays as well as books, a number of writers were making a career out of writing about blacks. The huge success of Van Vechten's book was added proof that Americans would support the work of any writer, white or black, who could "tell the Negro's story." So far, Van

Vechten had documented African-American life, as he knew it, in books, essays, and articles. In 1932, he found a new method.

Van Vechten began to take photographs of the artists, poets, and performers that he knew. Some of them were just beginning their careers. Others had already made quite a reputation for themselves, people such as Langston Hughes, Claude McKay, Aaron Douglas, Nella Larsen, and Zora Neale Hurston, to name a few. Van Vechten believed that people would want to learn more about the arts and events that he witnessed, so he collected all sorts of things to help explain the times he lived in: letters, newspaper and magazine clippings, theater programs, and photographs. The Library of Congress has more than 1,400 of Van Vechten's photographs that we can see now. Many of Van Vechten's photographs are still used as illustrations in books and magazines.

Van Vechten continued to write and photograph until he died in 1964 in New York City. Although some doubted his sincerity after hearing of his book *Nigger Heaven,* Van Vechten helped many of the great artists, writers, and performers of the Harlem Renaissance through his articles and by introducing them to people who could help their careers. Carl Van Vechten loved Harlem and the creative people who welcomed him into their lives. Van Vechten did far more than bring his white American and European friends to Harlem. He helped introduce Harlem, and African-American culture, to the world.

Patrons of the Harlem Renaissance

She wanted me to be primitive and know and feel the intuitions of the primitive. But, unfortunately, I did not feel the rhythms of the primitive surging through me, and so I could not live and write as though I did. I was only an American Negro—who had loved the surface of Africa and the rhythms of Africa—but I was not Africa. I was Chicago and Kansas City and Broadway and Harlem.

—Langston Hughes

Hughes's words tell us something important about the relationship between creative people and their patrons. A patron can give an artist the financial freedom to pursue his or her craft, and even the encouragement the artist needs to overcome difficulties. Patrons can also test an artist's resolve to be true to their own creative ideals.

Some patrons offer an artist support through purchasing the artist's work or by paying the artist's living and studying expenses. A patron may even pay for the artist to travel overseas for better training or to gain access to rare materials. But rarely does a patron do these things without demanding something in return. These demands oftentimes boil down to controlling

The Banjo Lesson, *by Henry Ossawa Tanner*

the kinds of works the artist creates. In the end, it is the artist who determines how much a patron affects their work.

Nancy Elizabeth Prophet refused patronage. Some, such as Henry Ossawa Tanner and Paul Robeson, were very cautious and limited their patron relationships. Others, such as Edmonia Lewis, Aaron Douglas, and Horace Pippin, remained fiercely independent of their patrons' "advice."

Individuals, organizations, and schools all played a part in nurturing the talented men and women of the Harlem Renaissance. Publishers, playwrights, recording companies, and the well-to-do white public were eager for the stories, paintings, and songs of authentic black life. Historian Nathan Huggins defined it this way:

> *After a history of struggle, of being an outcast, of being viewed with contempt or pity, the Negro was now courted and cultivated by cultured whites. How grand it was to be valued not for what one might become—the benevolent view of uplift—but for what was thought to be one's essential self, one's Negro-ness.*

What was this essential Negro-ness? Where did it come from? Arthur Schomburg wrote in his essay for Alain Locke's *The New Negro: An Interpretation* that it was a sense of reclaimed identity:

> *The Negro has been a man without a history because he has been considered a man without a worthy culture. But a new notion of the cultural attainment and potentialities of the African stocks has recently come about, partly through the corrective influence of the more scientific study of African institutions and early cultural history, partly through growing appreciation of the skill and beauty . . . of the African native crafts. . . . Already the Negro sees himself against a reclaimed background, in a perspective that will give pride and self-respect.*

Arthur Schomburg

Not all forms of patronage involve money. A patron can be a teacher or someone who is simply there to help when needed. Some individuals made great efforts to gather, and make available to all, the true history of the Negro's contributions and achievements from ancient days to the present. Arthur A. Schomburg amassed a large collection of African-American history, now housed in the Schomburg Center for Research in Black History and Culture in New York City. During his days as the curator of Harlem's 135th Street branch of the New York Public Library, he could be seen setting up a display of African masks, or hanging an exhibit of paintings by African-Americans. The Harlem library branch was a perfect location for the Harlem community to come and be inspired by the art of ancient times or the current works of New Negro talents. It also functioned as a patron of the Renaissance because poetry readings, art exhibits, and speeches by the leaders of the Renaissance were held there on a regular basis.

Alain Locke had an impressive collection of African art and was familiar with the collections held in Berlin, Germany, Paris, France and the extensive collection of Albert C. Barnes in the United States. Locke also introduced many talented African-Americans to wealthy people who could support their work.

Locke's educational achievements made him a very respectable man. His favorable opinion of an artist or a writer meant widespread publicity for that person in a number of important magazines. Often, Locke's opinion decided whether or not an African-American artist received a foundation grant.

Black colleges and universities were slow to recognize the importance of offering arts instruction. It was Alain Locke and W. E. B. Du Bois who pushed them to employ black art instructors and give exhibitions of African-American and African art. Through published writings, lectures, and personal relationships, Locke continued to influence black American art. However, he was not the only one to inspire young artists with the truth of noble African ancestry.

Charles Christopher Siefert, a black man from Barbados, in the West Indies, became a recognized expert on African and African-American history. Siefert's father, a plantation overseer, had books written by Englishmen before the spread of slavery. As a young boy, Siefert read these books. They gave a more honest account of African history than most books written after the height of the African slave trade. Siefert vowed to uncover the facts of history and bring them to light. He used to say, "You can be a better minister, a better Republican, Democrat, or Communist—whatever you want to be—if you first accept yourself and your history."

As Siefert prospered as a building contractor, he bought books, maps, African sculpture, and other artifacts. He established the Ethiopian School of Research History, where he taught small groups of artists, teachers, and college students. His lectures at the Harlem YMCA and at Fisk University were always crowded with listeners eager for the truth.

The truth, Siefert had learned, helped in dealing with the difficulties of being black in a white world. He was fond of saying, "If you came from a race of savages and cannibals, it is better to accept that than to hide it from yourself. But fortunately, history does not state that this is the case [for people of African descent]." He would then describe the courts, laws, wealth, and armies of the ancient kingdoms of Africa and their trade relations with the ancient Chinese, or their development of melting and casting iron and bronze, or their art and architecture.

Siefert simply knew more about Africa and its descendants than anyone else of his time. At one point, Marcus Garvey lived in Siefert's home to have access to Siefert's library and personal knowledge. But while the Renaissance men and women needed knowledge of their history, they also needed funding.

Charlotte Osgood Mason, the wealthy widow of Rufus Osgood Mason, supported a number of Harlem's most celebrated African-Americans. Zora Neale Hurston was given $200 a month and a car for two years, Langston Hughes's bills were paid for a summer so that he could finish his first novel, *Not without Laughter.* After she helped him to edit that work, she sent him a monthly allowance for the following year.

Mrs. Mason, secretive about her funding efforts, insisted that the recipients never tell her name and only call her "the godmother." For thirteen years, she paid for Alain Locke's annual trips to Europe. She was a personal friend to presidents, bankers, and famous scientists. But her financial aid came with a heavy price.

Hurston and Hughes read their work to the godmother and she was then the final judge of what was authentic, and true. She demanded that their works fit her idea of "primitive" or face her harsh criticism. In the end, she drove nearly all of them away. The primitive nature she sought to foster was not in their spirits; it existed only in her mind.

In the beginning, Hughes truly enjoyed the security of an "assured income" from someone who believed in him. He wrote, "No one else had ever been so thoughtful of me, or so interested in the things I wanted to do, or so kind and generous toward me." But when he realized he needed his freedom from her to write what he truly felt, her parting words were cold and cruel. Of their final meeting, he had this to say: "That beautiful room, that had been so full of light and help and understanding for me, suddenly became like a trap closing in, faster and faster, the room darker and darker, until the light went out with a sudden crash."

Black magazines such as A. Philip Randolph's *Messenger,* Du Bois and the NAACP's the *Crisis,* Charles S. Johnson and the Urban League's *Opportunity,* and black newspapers, large and small, gave exposure and held contests for African-American writers, poets, and artists. Caspar Holstein, who came from the Virgin Islands and rose to become the king of the Harlem numbers racket, provided the cash awards for the contests run by *Opportunity* magazine. But the organization that did the most to spread the word and work of the Harlem Renaissance artists was the Harmon Foundation.

Started by William E. Harmon and directed by Mary Beattie Brady after his death in 1928, the Harmon Foundation gave awards for outstanding achievement in eight fields, including literature and art. Through the foundation's art exhibitions, Brady helped hundreds of black Americans gain recognition as professional artists and documented their contributions in the exhibition catalogs. That documentation proved invaluable during the Great Depression of the 1930s, when these artists needed proof of professional status to join the ranks of artists employed by the federal arts programs.

Mary Brady, through the Harmon Foundation, sometimes bought paintings to give artists the money they needed to keep from being thrown out of their apartments. She saved the life's work of William H. Johnson when the storage company that was holding his work wanted to throw it all out because the storage bill had not been paid.

The Harmon Foundation made the American public aware of the amazing work being done by talented African-Americans all over the country. It also helped to get the art of black Americans into national museums and private collections, but it, too, had shortcomings.

The well-trained artists, some with impressive awards and recognition in Europe, were insulted to find that although Mary Brady had no training in art, she routinely refused to listen to their views and advice. Only Alain Locke, an advisor to the Harmon Foundation, was beyond her power to silence or control.

It was this unique combination of individuals, organizations, colleges and universities, YMCAs, and even the Harlem branch of the public library that made it possible to give the rich products of black American creativity to the world. Each had its own strengths and limitations, but each helped to make America conscious of the talents of its black citizens.

Yet even the most successful organization, the Harmon Foundation, held back the development of the artists it was trying to help. For creativity to flourish, it must have the freedom to define itself. The Harlem Renaissance patron, white or black, felt that he or she had the right to make the final decision on what was true, real, and authentically "Negro." This placed the artist in the heartbreaking position of struggling against both foes and friends in the search for a true expression of self.

Mary Edmonia Lewis

Sculptor
1845–?

Some praise me because I am a colored girl, and I don't want that kind of praise. I had rather you would point out my defects for that will teach me something.

Mary Edmonia Lewis, fiercely independent and determined, created sculptures that shine with a dignity that she herself was often denied in life. Her major themes included the spirituality of Native Americans and the brave men and women of the abolitionist movement

who fought to end slavery, women such as the Egyptian maiden Hagar, who—as related in the Bible story—struggled against the oppression of Abraham.

The dominant style of sculpture in Lewis's day was neoclassicism. It was difficult to show individual expression in this style because the artist had to conform the work to a very specific look. Not only did Lewis master that style, but she pushed it to carry the passion and emotion she felt for her subjects. Her daring choice to break out of that restrictive style established her as more than just the first great African-American sculptor. Despite racism and sexism she rose to be an innovator and leader of American sculpture, both in the United States and in Rome, Italy.

She was born on July 14, 1845, in Greenbush, New York, a small village across the Hudson River from Albany. Lewis's father was African-American, her mother a Chippewa Native American. Both of her parents died when she was around nine years old.

Edmonia and her older brother were taken in by two of her mother's sisters who lived with the Chippewa people near Niagara Falls in Canada. Living on the U.S.–Canadian border, she saw both fleeing slaves and the slave hunters that chased them. Because Edmonia looked more black than Native American, her aunts feared that as she grew older, the slave hunters might steal her away to be a slave in the United States.

Her older brother, Sunshine, fearful that their Native American way of life could not outlast the white man's interference, headed for the California gold rush in the 1850s. He hoped to make it rich and ensure their continued freedom.

Sunshine returned after a few years having, indeed, become wealthy from his adventures in California. He insisted on paying for Lewis to get an education. But Lewis had difficulties in school because the English consonants *r, l, f, v, x* and the word *the* are not part of the Chippewa language, so she could not pronounce them. Still, she learned to read and write and eventually was accepted at Oberlin College, near Cleveland, Ohio, in 1859.

While there, she realized that she had a talent for drawing and worked hard to improve her skill. She enjoyed sketching the small copies of Greek and Roman sculptures that the school had. But she had difficulty making friends because she still had trouble speaking English.

Lewis had been in Oberlin only a few months when John Brown and his followers seized the Harpers Ferry arsenal in hopes of starting a slave revolt. John Brown, the famous white abolitionist, had family ties to Oberlin, which was a center of support for the abolition of slavery. When he and his men were caught, tried, and hanged for their actions the townspeople were outraged. About one-fourth of the town's residents were free African-Americans, but many of the small towns around Oberlin did not share their views on slavery. It was a terrifying lesson to Lewis about what can happen to people who actively fought against slavery.

During Lewis's third year at Oberlin, two white girls she had become friends with accused her of putting a love potion called Spanish fly in their drinks before they went on a sledding date with two boys. Oberlin had strict rules forbidding males and females from being alone together, and the case was taken very seriously. Lewis was taken to court and charged with poisoning.

She was hurt that her so-called friends would spread such lies about her. Some people in the neighboring towns who hated blacks—and hated Oberlin because the school admitted women, blacks, and Native Americans—stirred up more trouble and threatened violence.

Lewis was to be defended by a young black lawyer named John Mercer Langston, himself an Oberlin graduate. Before the trial could begin, however, Lewis was grabbed during the night, taken out to a field, savagely beaten, and left for dead in the snow.

Fortunately, she survived the ordeal, and Langston's brilliant defense cleared her of any wrongdoing. But the betrayal, near-fatal beating, and mean-spirited teasing that followed left her unable to trust anyone again. This had far-reaching effects on her artistic development. She found herself unable to accept advice or constructive criticism from whites which would have helped her artistic progress. Instead she took the road of slow progress by trial and error on her own.

Even with that incident behind her, she became the scapegoat on campus and was under constant scrutiny. Since there was no real reason to expel her, Mrs. Marianne Dascomb, the head of the ladies' department, simply refused to accept Lewis's registration for her fourth and final year of study. So Lewis, determined to prove how wrong they were, left for Boston to become a sculptor.

Lewis chose the renowned Edward A. Brackett as her teacher because of the remarkable bust he sculpted of John Brown. She insisted on learning on her own by studying his works and learning to copy them. She soon was selling small plaster medallions of John Brown and other abolitionists to support herself while she learned.

By teaching herself and selling her works, Lewis managed to save enough money to finance a trip to Florence, Italy, to study the sculptures of Michelangelo and Donatello. She had been working in a realistic style in Boston, which lent personality and character to her portraits. But for serious sculptors, neoclassicism was considered the highest form of artistic expression.

Neoclassical means that artists followed the "classical" forms of Greek sculpture, based on ancient Greek ideals of perfection and beauty. Natural human imperfections and individual character were covered up. It was a difficult style, but since Edmonia sculpted blacks, whites, and Native Americans, she hoped that it could best show the basic universal humanity of all the races.

Lewis soon learned that Rome was where the bulk of American tourists went—the people most likely to buy her portraits of abolitionists and copies of famous Roman sculptures. She arrived in Rome in 1866. Although she soon made a strong reputation for herself, she was constantly challenged to prove that she had actually done the work. Some customers even refused to buy unless they could watch her work. They simply could not believe that people of African descent were capable of creating fine art. This was a widely held belief and, tragically, had even been stated in speeches by one of America's founding fathers, Thomas Jefferson.

While in Rome, Lewis created a statue of a man and woman to celebrate the Emancipation Proclamation—the document that officially freed American slaves. The sculpture was completed in 1868 and titled *Forever Free*. It was the first sculpture by an African-American to celebrate that historic occasion, and Lewis used the opportunity to break from the classical mode.

While the female in the piece is idealized in the Greek tradition, the male is clearly a realistic portrayal of an African-American. He is obviously of mixed race, which pointed out certain disgraceful facts about slavery in America.

Lewis also created sensitive works on Native American subjects. She combined classical features with realistic details that she recalled from her days of living with her mother's people in Canada.

Although Lewis experimented with bold sculptural statements of realism, she returned often to the classical style because that was what sold. Her most daring break with classicism, though, came in 1875—a life-size, 2-ton statue titled *The Death of Cleopatra* that was shown at the 1876 Centennial Exposition in Philadelphia.

Art was supposed to be noble, and anything that dealt with death was to be done as idealized "noble suffering." That meant there was to be no

Forever Free, *by Mary Edmonia Lewis*

sign of pain, sorrow, or regret. Concerning Lewis's *The Death of Cleopatra*, the artist Walter J. Clark wrote:

> [T]his is not a beautiful work, but it is a very original and striking one and it deserve[s] particular comment, as its ideals [are] so radically different. . . . The effects of death are represented with such skill as to be absolutely repellent. Apart from all questions of taste, however, the striking qualities of the work are undeniable, and it could only have been produced by a sculptor of genuine endowments.

Lewis's daring realism became the talk of the Centennial Exposition. Although it shocked many, the critics praised her. The *Oberlin Review* bragged that the "renowned sculptor" had taken her first art lessons at their college. For Lewis, this was apt revenge for the pain and humiliation people in Oberlin had caused her sixteen years before.

It is a sad fact, though, that the middle-class blacks of Philadelphia did not support her or her work. In an interview with African Methodist Episcopal (AME) minister and educator John P. Sampson, she revealed that instead of encouraging her, they only criticized her work.

In her blunt way, she told the minister that she would not stay where black people stood around imitating the prejudices of white folk. "I am going back to Italy," she declared, "to do something for the race—something that will excite the admiration of the other races of the earth."

Of all the American artists working in Rome during the 1860s and 1870s, Mary Edmonia Lewis alone reached beyond the limitations of neoclassicism to portray a uniquely American expression of her times. She created works with passion and a sense of individual style. The date and place of her death are unknown, but her life's work, a testament to honor both sides of her ancestry, led the way for the next generation of African-Americans.

Henry Ossawa Tanner

Painter
1859–1937

The American obsession [with race] has driven me out of the country . . . while I cannot sing our national hymn, 'land of liberty,' etc., still deep down in my heart I love it and am sometimes sad that I cannot live where my heart is.

Henry Ossawa Tanner was born small and frail on June 21, 1859, in Pittsburgh, Pennsylvania. His mother, Sarah Miller Tanner, had been born a slave in Virginia. Henry's father, Benjamin Tucker Tanner, "a third-generation Pittsburgher," had recently become a minister of the African Methodist Episcopal (AME) Church.

Pittsburgh, less than 100 miles north of slave territory, was known to have violent, proslavery groups. That did not stop Reverend Tanner from making his home one of the stations on the Underground Railroad and helping slaves to escape.

Henry's father became a strong leader during the Civil War and the following period known as Reconstruction. In 1864, Henry's family moved to Philadelphia where the AME church had its headquarters, and Reverend Tanner preached at its founding church, "Mother Bethel."

At home and in Mother Bethel, Henry heard the plans and preachings of the great AME leaders. Their stories, challenges, faith, and pride in being black inspired and reassured Henry.

Reverend Tanner realized that his work often kept him away from his family while Henry was growing up. When he came home, he and Henry would take long walks in Fairmont Park so that he could get to know his son better. On one of these walks they saw an artist painting a landscape.

Father and son watched the artist turn the flat, white canvas into a beautiful scene—a colorful wooded hill, a stretch of cool green grass, and a mighty elm tree. Henry decided on the spot that he must learn to paint. That night his mother gave him fifteen cents for materials. The next day he returned to that same place and made his first painting.

Henry loved painting, mixing and experimenting with paints of different colors. His parents did not understand his intense desire to be an artist, but for eighteen years they helped support his efforts, both financially and emotionally.

Because of racial prejudice, Henry had a difficult time finding artists willing to train a Negro. Mostly, he struggled along on his own until his talent gained him entry into the Pennsylvania Academy of Fine Arts, then the finest art school in the United States.

Thomas Eakins, who believed in painting things as they really were, rather than romantic notions of them, was the director of the academy. He took an interest in Tanner, and Tanner adopted many of Eakins's techniques and methods. They remained friends for life.

Unfortunately, Tanner had to face racism even in the academy. One such incident involved Tanner being tied to his easel by a group of white students, carried out to the middle of Broad Street, and left there. Such cruel treatment and jokes by students eventually drove him to quit the academy.

He tried to support himself as an artist, but was barely able to afford brushes and paint. After eight years of this frustration, a prominent white couple—Bishop and Mrs. Joseph C. Hartzell of the Methodist Episcopal Church in Cincinnati—became interested in his work. In 1890, they arranged for Tanner to teach art at Clark University in Atlanta, making him the first African-American painter to teach at a black college.

Through the Hartzells, Tanner was able to study at the Académie Julien in Paris, France. He made many friends there and felt a freedom he had never known in America. He was forced to return to America, however, to recuperate from typhoid fever. While he recovered, he thought about the love and support his family gave him—of how they also longed for his success.

Few white Americans were aware of this side of African-American life. Tanner felt compelled to show the warmth and love of black Americans despite the abusive conditions that they had to endure. He created two paintings that would later be hailed by the best of the Harlem Renaissance for their beauty and their realistic views of African-American life. Those two paintings were *The Banjo Lesson* and *The Thankful Poor.*

Both paintings were true-to-life scenes of tenderness and love that showed humanity at its best—an older generation caring for and teaching a younger one. They were seen as powerful evidence against claims that

Tanner painting in his studio

blacks were a lower form of human than whites. *The Banjo Lesson* also celebrated the music of African-Americans through their invented instrument
—the banjo.

The Banjo Lesson was accepted at the Paris Salon of 1894, a notable
accomplishment. Tanner knew, though, that the judges of the Paris Salon
felt that scenes of everyday life were genre paintings, and not art of the
highest rank. In their opinion, important art dealt with great historical
events or classical themes. If Tanner wished to show that blacks could earn
the highest honors of artistic recognition, then he needed subjects that
could command such attention.

When Tanner returned to Paris, he returned to his roots—the Bible stories that had given him hope through all his difficulties. Those wonderful stories of triumph over oppression had sustained generations of African-Americans. James Weldon Johnson once stated:

> It is not possible to estimate the sustaining influence that the story of the trials and tribulations of Jews as related in the Old Testament exerted upon the Negro. This story at once caught and fired the imagination of the Negro bards, and they sang, sang their hungry listeners into a firm faith that as God saved Daniel in the lion's den, so would He save them; as God preserved the Hebrew children in a fiery furnace, so He would preserve them; as God delivered Israel out of bondage in Egypt, so would He deliver them.

Tanner's painting skills were impressive and he continued to experiment with color and light to lend emotion and power to his works. His painting *Daniel in the Lions' Den* won much praise and an honorable mention in the Paris Salon of 1896. Because of Tanner's upbringing and deep emotional connection to the stories, his biblical scenes were extraordinary portrayals of the power and mystery of faith and miracles.

Tanner's painting *The Raising of Lazarus* not only received a medal. It also received international critical acclaim and was even purchased by the French government! The whole world knew that an African-American had won one of the highest honors in the art world—an honor that only a handful of American artists had achieved. In the great salon halls, filled with thousands of paintings, Tanner's painting attracted crowds. This wonderful achievement would be an enormous inspiration to the next generation of artists.

Though he was criticized for not returning to the United States to paint black life, nearly every black American artist who traveled to Europe visited him and was encouraged by him. Tanner continued to paint the scenes that had given him strength and courage all his life. His fame spread, and the sales of his works grew dramatically. In 1924, the French government appointed him a Chevalier (knight) of the Legion of Honor, the highest honor awarded to a civilian in France.

Though he tried to live again in the United States, prejudice forced him and his wife, Jessie Olssen, to go back to France. Tanner just could not bear to see his son scarred by the racism that he knew only too well.

Tanner died in his sleep on May 25, 1937, in his Paris apartment. His incredible achievements were a source of pride and inspiration to all African-Americans, and especially to black American artists. Though he had been criticized for not painting more scenes of black life, Tanner's paintings portrayed something just as important—the source of African-Americans' spiritual strength.

May Howard Jackson

Sculptor
1877–1931

*A*fter May Howard Jackson's death in 1931, W. E. B. Du Bois wrote:

With her sensitive soul she needed encouragement and contacts and delicate appreciation. Instead of this, she ran into the shadows of the Color Line. Problems of race, class, of poverty and family may affect different persons quite differently. . . . In the case of May Howard Jackson . . . [i]t made her at once bitter and fierce with energy, cynical of praise and above all at odds with life and people. She met with rebuffs in her attempts to study, and in her attempts at exhibition, in her chosen ideal of portraying the American mulatto type; with her own friends and people she faced continual doubt as to whether it was worthwhile and what it was all for.

Difficulty and hardship are a natural part of life, yet we often wonder why some people don't just give up when their chosen path seems impossible. We watch them struggle in vain and marvel that they continue to pick themselves up and keep right on trying.

For artists, it seems that there is no other way. The drive to create cannot be set aside or ignored. An artist cannot be told to produce only "acceptable" images. May Howard Jackson could not ignore the artist within her. Her sculptures were honest and sincere comments on race and history in America. But America was not ready for such a forthright vision.

May was born in Philadelphia, Pennsylvania, in 1877—the same year and in the same city as sculptor Meta Warrick Fuller. May is noted as being one of the first African-American sculptors to break away from the popular European art traditions. In her sculptures, she chose America's racial problems as her subject matter.

Jackson began her art studies at Professor J. Liberty-Tadd's art school. She continued her studies at the Pennsylvania Academy of Fine Arts but was unable to pursue further education overseas or at home in the United States. That did not stop her from following her own ideas of what was important and essential in art.

Jackson chose portrait sculpture as her means of expression. This choice was important. Portraiture was the most direct approach available to African-Americans in the fight against the insulting stereotyped images that white American artists and illustrators had been making for decades. Those stereotyped portrayals included big red lips, bug eyes, watermelons, and chickens. They showed blacks as lazy, lustful, primitive, cowardly, and superstitious—more of a joke than a human being. Jackson challenged those images with the strength of her sculpted portraits

Portraits do more than record the way a person looks. Portraits are also ways of showing what is true about all people by showing what is true about one person. In one man, woman, or child, we can see the basic human traits that are common to all men, women, and children. Jackson's importance is that she was one of the first sculptors to use portraits to proclaim the humanity of African-Americans. Her humanistic approach has been used and refined by African-American artists ever since.

Jackson has been described as a "volunteer Negro." Because of her mixed ancestry, she could have passed as a white woman. Jackson was fiercely proud of her black heritage, but she would not deny the full scope of her ancestry either.

Melville Herskovits, in his contribution to Alain Locke's book *The New Negro: An Interpretation,* stated that "the fact remains that the vast majority of Negroes in America are of mixed ancestry." Jackson's sculptures called attention to the people who are considered between black and white. In those days, the polite yet demeaning terms used were mulatto, quadroon, octaroon, and many others depending on the amount of white ancestry a person had. The larger society, however, continued to think of the races as strictly separate, all-black or all-white. They also felt, very strongly, that the races should remain separate.

At first glance, Jackson's portrait *Head of a Negro Child* appears to be a study of a white child. The thick, straight hair does not seem to fit with the "Negro" part of the title. Looking closer, however, we see a wide nose and full lips. We also see the sad face of a child who just might be wondering why some people treat him differently or call him names.

Though Jackson won both awards and critical acclaim, she found that family, friends, and the general black public did not appreciate her efforts. This was a source of great pain for her that eventually turned to bitterness. In addition, she had a hard time finding exhibitions in which to show her work. State fairs were just about the only places for black artists to exhibit their work in those days. But Jackson never gave up and never stopped sculpting.

Jackson's talent was recognized by some of the most important black leaders of her day—W. E. B. Du Bois and Alain Leroy Locke. She was a judge for several of the Harmon Foundation's annual exhibitions. And when a young orphan Sargent Claude Johnson came to live with May and her husband, Sherman William Jackson, her sculpture had a profound impact on the boy. Sargent later became a sculptor himself.

Jackson's influence can be seen in Sargent's sculpture portrait *Elizabeth Gee*. It has much of the expression and the quiet sadness of Jackson's *Head of a Negro Child*. Despite her difficulties and lack of support, May Howard Jackson remained true to her artistic feelings and beliefs. As a result, her works have a strength and honesty about them that inspired generations of sculptors and painters. Those artists built on her example and portrayed African-Americans with realism and integrity.

Meta Vaux Warrick Fuller

Sculptor
1877–1968

The Negro has been emancipated [freed] from slavery but not from the curse of race hatred and prejudice.

Meta Vaux Warrick Fuller was born into the black, middle-class community of Philadelphia, Pennsylvania, in 1877. Slavery in America had been abolished for only fourteen years. Her father, a barber, and her mother, a beautician, were able to provide her with a much better education than most African-Americans could get at that time, especially women.

Meta studied for five years at the Pennsylvania Museum and School of Industrial Arts (now the Philadelphia College of Art). While there, she won first prize for a metal sculpture of Christ on the cross. It was unusual in that it portrayed Jesus' face with an expression of agony. Strong emotions such as that were rarely shown in art at that time.

It was felt then that art should be different from nature, more perfect and ideal. This style was known as neoclassicism—"neo," meaning "new" and "classic" because it was based on the Greek and Roman ideas of art, the classical era of art history.

Strong emotions such as fear, anger, and pain were softened by the artist and presented as noble suffering. But Meta was interested in people's emotions. She wanted viewers to be touched by the feelings of her subjects. As her friend Velma J. Hoover explained,

> *At the turn of the century in the United States, most black persons were afraid to publicly verbalize the pain, sorrow and despair of the black experience, and a woman was seldom expected to voice any opinion at all. Meta Fuller found creative expression of these feelings through her sculpture, and her works were "powerful" because she was expressing very real pain, sorrow and despair.*

Meta went to Paris in 1899 to continue her studies in art and enrolled at the famous Colarossi Academy. She met Auguste Rodin, one of Europe's greatest sculptors, and studied under him.

Meta made a reputation for herself in Paris as a talented sculptor in the new style of romantic realism. She exhibited her work in the renowned S. Bing's gallery of modern art and design. Romantic realism meant that instead of round, smooth, and polished surface textures like those in neoclassical sculpture, Meta's sculptures had rough surfaces and less emphasis on ideal beauty. She concentrated on showing her ideas of the subject's character and emotions. For Meta, expressing the truth about how things really were was more important than traditional ideas of Greek beauty.

She returned to America in 1905 and exhibited the sculptures she created while in Paris. At that time, many African-American artists showed their work at state fairs and exhibitions. Some state fairs even gave commissions to black artists. Critics called her sculptures gruesome, shocking, and macabre because she dealt with powerful themes such as death, war, and anguish.

In 1907, Meta received a commission from the Jamestown Tercentennial Exposition to portray the advancement of blacks since the end of slavery. In 1913, she created a sculpture for the New York State Emancipation Proclamation Commission.

In 1909, Meta married Dr. Solomon Fuller. He was a psychologist and neurologist from Liberia, in Africa. They settled in Framingham, Massachusetts, near Boston. In Framingham, against the wishes of her husband, Fuller built herself a sculpture studio with her own hands to continue the work she loved.

Fuller created the bronze sculpture *Ethiopia Awakening* in 1914. This work went on to become the symbol of the New Negro movement, because it captured the spirit of the Harlem Renaissance.

Ethiopia is a country in Africa, but the name was used in ancient times to mean all African peoples. Fuller's sculpture portrays a beautiful African woman, her head turned to the left. She appears to be awakening from a long, deep sleep. She wears the headdress of a queen of Egypt, and from her waist to her feet she is wrapped like a mummy. Her right hand, hovering above her heart, holds one end of the cloth that binds her legs. Slowly, the African queen is unwrapping the funeral cloth that keeps her from moving freely.

Fuller had related all African peoples to the image of Africa as a sleeping African queen who would one day awaken to reclaim her glory. She connected Africa's glorious past with the present-day condition of African-descended peoples all over the world, bound up in the confining cloth of racism. But Fuller expressed hope for the future by portraying Ethiopia as awakening to a new sense of self-awareness and casting off the limitations of prejudice.

Fuller became the first artist to demonstrate a link between Africa and modern African-Americans. Her statue expressed the hope that by claiming this connection, African-Americans could reclaim their history and beauty and raise themselves to new heights of glory. This would become a central idea of the Harlem Renaissance.

Fuller continued to stress the connection between African-Americans and Africa. The black American elite indeed heralded her marriage to the famous African physician Solomon Fuller as a prophetic linking of the two cultures. She continued creating sculptures, many of which were based upon African folktales and black American songs. Fuller died on March 13, 1968.

Meta Vaux Warrick Fuller stands in history as the first African-American artist to assert that Africa and black Americans were connected, and that the connection had meaning and importance for the present and the future. Before her example, black artists in America and Europe portrayed the same kinds of images as white artists. Some notable exceptions are Edmonia Lewis's sculpture *Forever Free* (1867) and Henry Ossawa Tanner's two paintings *The Banjo Lesson* (1893) and *The Thankful Poor* (1894).

Not only did Fuller bring a new artistic movement to America—romantic realism—but she also offered African-Americans a source of pride and identity that was not rooted in European traditions—their rich African heritage. It would be another ten years before a young Aaron Douglas built upon the legacy that Fuller started with *Ethiopia Awakening.*

Nancy Elizabeth Prophet

Sculptor
1890–1960

W. E. B. Du Bois wrote of Nancy Elizabeth Prophet, "She never whined or made any excuses for herself. . . . She never submitted to patronage, cringed to the great or begged the small. She worked."

Concerning her life and work, she once stated, "[My education came from] the college of serious thought and bitter experience, situated on the campus of poverty and ambition."

It has been said that Nancy Elizabeth Prophet felt her sculptures were distinctly unracial. But her powerful expressions of noble conflict suggest that more of her life as an African-American woman of mixed race was present in her work than she may have realized.

She was born in Warwick, Rhode Island, on March 19, 1890. She described her father as being a Negro of mixed race and her mother as a Narragansett Indian. Her parents were poor and did not approve of her ambition to become an artist. They thought it was a most impractical dream for a Negro in those times and especially for a Negro woman. They did everything they could to discourage her. Even relatives and family friends advised her to choose something more sensible. They suggested she become a servant for white folks or a teacher for black children, because those were the only jobs open for a woman of color. But Nancy knew what she wanted and refused to settle for less.

For four years, Prophet worked and saved so that she could attend the Rhode Island School of Design. She began with drawing and painting, and her specialty was portraiture. She then learned to sculpt busts in wood, stone and bronze. Nancy loved creating realistic portraits in clay, wood, and stone. She worked hard with nimble fingers or hammer and chisel to create portraits that showed individual personalities. Prophet wanted her sculptures to seem alive with emotion.

While she was still a student at the Rhode Island School of Design, Prophet met a young black man named Francis Ford and they married. In 1918, she graduated and found a gallery in nearby Newport, Rhode Island, that was interested in showing her sculptures. The gallery had a policy, however, of not allowing Negroes to mingle socially with their clients. They could accept her wonderful sculptures, but they could not accept the black woman herself in their gallery.

Prophet was furious and refused to show her work there. She went to

New York City, but each gallery there had the same condition—her work was welcome, but she was not. Nancy realized that the only way to be accepted in her own country was to first make a name for herself in the great art center of Paris, France. Then these galleries would not dare to tell her she was not as welcome as her sculptures.

Again, she worked and saved to reach her goal. Somehow she saved the enormous sum of $350 and set off for Paris in 1922. Prophet was immediately accepted into the renowned Ecole des Beaux Arts. She was determined to make the most of this rare opportunity.

In her daily journal, she wrote of her first days at the famous French school, "I worked away on my first piece with a dogged determination. . . . I remember how sure I was that it was going to be a living thing, a master stroke, how my arms felt as I swung them up to put on a piece of clay." But Nancy had very little money to live on. In that same journal entry, she talked of her hunger. She was sharing a studio with a Frenchwoman and her dog. Prophet was so hungry that she stole a piece of meat and a potato from the dog's plate and ate it ravenously.

Prophet's marriage to Ford did not last long. She invited him to join her in Paris. In her journal she wrote of his arrival that he was "helpless . . . without ambition." Prophet was a woman filled with drive and determination, and she could neither understand nor tolerate this lack in her husband.

While in France, she met other black Americans who had left America, as she had done, to further their careers. In fact, there was a whole community of African-Americans who either lived in France or visited frequently. Most notably, there was W. E. B. Du Bois, the influential activist and social critic, the talented young poet Countee Cullen, and Henry Ossawa Tanner, a black painter of international fame. Countee Cullen stated that though Prophet lived in Paris, she closely followed events in black America and maintained her racial pride and identity.

Prophet's talent earned her quite a reputation, and Du Bois, in particular, was impressed by her powerful, realistic style. For ten years, Prophet remained in Paris, where her life-size sculptures, often in marble, won glowing reviews from the French art critics.

She had many successful shows both in France and in America before she finally returned to the United States in 1932. Ten years after the Newport gallery had insulted her, she was invited to exhibit at the Newport Art Association, a place where millionaires came to view her work. Also in 1932, Prophet won first prize at the Twenty-First Annual Newport Art Association Exhibition with her wood sculpture *Discontent*. Countee Cullen described that piece as "so powerful in the red polished cowl that envelops it . . . that it might stand for the very spirit of revolt and rebellion."

In 1934, W. E. B. Du Bois persuaded Prophet to teach at Atlanta University in Georgia. She went on from there to teach at Spelman College. Prophet enjoyed giving young artists the encouragement that she had rarely received.

Prophet continued teaching at Spelman until 1944 when her father became ill, and she went back to Rhode Island to look after him. She remained there for the rest of her life, living quietly and continuing to sculpt. She died of a heart attack in 1960.

The outstanding works of Nancy Elizabeth Prophet mirrored her own proud way of life—each portrait was a sensitively chiseled study of "noble conflict" with faces that reflected pride, grim lessons, and unshakable determination. Prophet never needed to claim a racial intent for her art. Her struggles and triumphs as a woman of "mixed race" are forever written in the stone, bronze, and wood of each carefully sculpted face.

Aaron Douglas

Painter
1899–1979

echnique in itself is not enough. It is important for the artist to develop the power to convey emotion . . . the artist's technique, no matter how brilliant it is, should never obscure his vision.

From when he was a child, Aaron Douglas loved to draw. His mother encouraged him by hanging up his drawings and paintings and telling others of her son's talent. One day Aaron's mother came home from working for the Malvane family with a magazine. The Malvanes were very interested in art and had even started a museum at Washburn University in Topeka, Kansas. The magazine was a present for Aaron. Inside he saw a reproduction of a painting by the world-famous black artist Henry Ossawa Tanner. It was a scene of Christ and Nicodemus meeting on a rooftop in the moonlight. "I remember the painting very well," Aaron later said. "I spent hours poring over it, and that helped to lead me to deciding to become an artist."

Aaron was born on May 26, 1899, in Topeka, Kansas, to Aaron and Elizabeth Douglas. He was fortunate to have had a better formal education than most black artists during the Harlem Renaissance. He studied fine arts at the University of Nebraska in Lincoln—including drawing, painting, and art history. He recalled "I was the only black student there. Because I was sturdy and friendly, I became popular with both faculty and students."

Douglas graduated from the University of Nebraska in 1922 and received a bachelor of fine arts degree from the University of Kansas in 1923 where he also studied psychology and education. He went on to teach art at Lincoln High School in Topeka, Kansas, from 1923 to the summer of 1925. Douglas was the first art teacher the school ever had. While teaching there, he received letters from friends in New York City talking about the great things going on there. Those letters, with their stories of progress, pride, and advances being made, convinced Aaron that New York City or, more precisely, Harlem was the place for a young black artist to make a way for himself. That same year he moved to Harlem.

Douglas arrived in New York without a place to stay, so his friend Ethel Ray Nance let him sleep on her couch until he could find work and a place of his own. She introduced Aaron to her employer, Charles S. Johnson. Johnson, a sociologist—a person who studies people and their social behaviors—was editor of the widely read and respected *Opportunity* magazine, published by the Urban League.

Johnson also introduced Douglas to German artist Winold Reiss, who was known for his realistic portraits of blacks and Native Americans. For this reason, as well as for his modern, progressive style, Alain Locke invited Reiss to design and illustrate the "Harlem" issue of *Survey Graphic* magazine.

Reiss made Douglas question traditional academic painting and suggested that Douglas look to African art for a way to express his racial commitment. Fortunately for Douglas, he also met an art collector from Philadelphia named Albert C. Barnes.

Barnes was one of the wealthy white supporters of black art in the 1920s. He had an extensive collection of West African sculpture as well as the latest works by European modernists such as Picasso, Gauguin, and Matisse. Douglas was deeply influenced by what he saw in Barnes's collection and used what he learned to create his own painting style. It combined the angles and simple forms seen in African sculpture with a sense of progress and a modern African-American identity.

Locke and Reiss asked Douglas to provide illustrations for the expanded book version of the "Harlem" *Survey Graphic* issue titled *The New Negro: An Interpretation.* The book was widely hailed as the defining literature of the black Renaissance, and Douglas's illustrations were a part of that definition.

Douglas soon had requests for illustrations from such magazines as *Vanity Fair, Harare's,* the NAACP's the *Crisis,* the Urban League's *Opportunity,* and *Theatre Arts Monthly.* There were also requests to illustrate a number of other important books of the time such as James Weldon Johnson's *God's Trombones.* These publications made Aaron Douglas the most widely recognized artist of the Harlem Renaissance.

Douglas's unique style and the popularity of his dancing figures earned him a commission from the wealthy owner of Club Ebony in New York

City. He paid Douglas $700, a very large sum at that time, to paint a mural in the nightclub. It was a big hit, and the popularity of that mural led to more commissions for such places as Chicago's Sherman Hotel, Harlem's YMCA, and the Erasto Milo Library of Fisk University. The Countee Cullen Branch of the New York Public Library holds Douglas's most famous mural, *The Aspects of Negro Life*.

In *The Aspects of Negro Life*, Douglas took on the huge task of retelling the story of African-American history from Africa, through slavery and Reconstruction, to the New Negro of the 1920s:

> *I tried to keep my forms very stark and geometric with my main emphasis on the human body. I tried to portray everything not in a realistic but abstract way—simplified and abstract as . . . in the spirituals. In fact, I used the starkness of the old spirituals as my model—and at the same time I tried to make my painting modern.*

Although Douglas had received financial help from the wealthy patron Charlotte Osgood Mason, he soon learned that her controlling nature was too high a price to pay for her support. Alfred C. Barnes, the noted collector of modern art and founder of an art school in Merion, Pennsylvania, offered Douglas a scholarship and stipend to attend the school in 1928. When she learned of it, Mrs. Mason tried to stop Douglas from attending. She told him that he would ruin his "natural, primitive" instincts with further art instruction. Douglas ignored her demands, and she ended her financial support.

By saving what he could from his mural sales, Douglas paid for himself and his wife, Alta Mae Sawyer, to go to Paris for his studies. Douglas first attended the Académie de la Grande Chaumière, and then the Académie Scandinave. While in Paris, Douglas met Palmer Hayden. Hayden introduced him to the artist that had inspired Douglas as a boy—Henry Ossawa Tanner. Douglas was thrilled to talk to his idol about his own studies and painting theories. Tanner was very encouraging to both Hayden and Douglas.

Douglas and his wife returned to America, out of money but rich in experience. He secured more mural commissions, but times were hard in the early 1930s because of the depressed economy.

Discrimination against black artists in the government's Works Progress Administration (WPA), an agency set up to supply work and materials for artists during the depression, prompted Aaron to take an active role in the fight for equal opportunity. Douglas was elected as the first president of the Harlem Artists' Guild and helped to win recognition for black artists in the WPA. Douglas's apartment on Edgecomb Avenue became one of the gathering places for artists and writers in the latter days of the Harlem Renaissance. It was a place to meet and talk about the issues and challenges that they shared.

In 1936, in a speech at the first American Artists Congress concerning what the Negro artist should paint, Douglas said:

> *Our chief concern has been to establish and maintain recognition of our essential humanity, in other words, complete social and political equality. This has been a difficult fight as we have been the constant object of attack by all manner of propaganda from nursery rhymes to false scientific racial theories.*

Aaron Douglas and others in the arts fought back against the "propaganda" and "false racial theories" with the power of their creative works. His unique vision of black life and history celebrated the ability of African-Americans to change and overcome hardships. He painted a history that was more than a list of great events; it was a record of black people's spirit and will—a blending of the ancestral legacy and the modern black American that Alain Locke had called for in his landmark book *The New Negro: An Interpretation.*

Douglas died on February 2, 1979, in Nashville, Tennessee. His strong, unique way of seeing Africans and African-Americans is the one most closely associated with the Harlem Renaissance.

James Van Der Zee

Photographer and Photojournalist
1886–1983

James Van Der Zee's photographs dismissed the racist stereotypes that labeled black people as ignorant and inferior to whites. His pictures were a mirror that showed the people of Harlem, and all African-Americans, that their dreams had come true: they were prosperous, educated, cultured, and right in step with modern times.

Born in 1886 in Lenox, Massachusetts, which was surrounded by resort hotels and mountain estates, James worked at the Hotel Aspinwall as a waiter. At the age of twelve, he sold twenty packets of perfume and won a prize—his first camera. Photography was simply a hobby. He loved to play the violin and the piano, and he also enjoyed painting. In 1906, Van Der Zee moved to Harlem and married his first wife, Kate Brown. They moved to Virginia for a short time, where Van Der Zee worked as a busboy and part-time photographer. He was eager to move back to New York where he could resume his original plan—to be a musician. That same year the newlyweds returned to New York and James organized the Harlem Orchestra. For a short time, he lived the life of a musician. He played the piano for numerous public and private gatherings and sat in with popular musicians of the era like Fletcher Henderson.

Though Van Der Zee was no longer working as a photographer, he nurtured his talent and emerged a self-taught genius and one of the first African-American photographers of the twentieth century. Van Der Zee had a difficult time making ends meet on a musician's wages. He is quoted as saying, "I got to eat three times a day—I might look into photographing again." So he took a job as a darkroom technician at Gertz Department Store in Newark, where he earned $5 a day.

At Gertz, Van Der Zee was often left alone and had to act as the photographer. He used this opportunity to test out ideas for props and poses that made his clients' portraits unique. He would use objects in his pictures, posing his subjects with a book, a cigarette, or flowers. People loved Van Der Zee's style so much that the young photographer was able to open his own studio, Guarantee Photo. The business was on 135th Street, right in the center of Harlem activity and the cultural explosion of the Renaissance. His business boomed throughout the 1920s, and by the early 1930s he had opened a second studio on Lenox Avenue.

Among his countless subjects were political activists, artists, writers, musicians, actors—the crème de la crème of the New Negro movement. James Van Der Zee had the unique experience of being a part of every aspect of Harlem—organizations, high-society parties, marriages, births, and even deaths. One of his most famous photographs is a shot of the 369th Infantry Regiment of African-American soldiers when they returned from France and proudly marched up Fifth Avenue.

Like most artists of the Harlem Renaissance, Van Der Zee did not want to follow anyone else's rules when it came to his craft. He wanted the freedom to create pictures his own way. He said, "I was never satisfied with things the way they looked. I liked working with a big portrait camera so I could make changes. . . . That was my style, though. Not like other portrait photographers where all you saw was more faces that looked the same." Van Der Zee knew how to manipulate photographs to create the desired effect. He could remove wrinkles and blemishes, and he could even add hair upon request. A few members of the photography community criticized the changes he made in his photographs, but what other people said did not affect James Van Der Zee's style. He used painted backdrops to create different moods and settings. Van Der Zee thrived on exploring photography as an art form.

He was also a great photojournalist, able to capture real-life events that made history. Van Der Zee was one of the hardest-working men of the Harlem Renaissance. He was never confined to his studio. He would go on location to take his photographs when called. At the height of Marcus Garvey's popularity Van Der Zee was appointed the official photographer for Garvey's United Negro Improvement Association. Through his photographs, he preserved the group's big parades, which featured the uniformed Black Cross nurses and Black Eagle Flying Corps, among others.

After the 1940s, smaller and less expensive cameras were introduced, and people began to take their own pictures. Though his business declined, the fact remained that no one could take a portrait like James Van Der Zee. He continued to make a living taking portraits and retouching photographs for others.

Unlike many artists and writers of his time, Van Der Zee lived long enough to be fully honored for his artistry and his thorough documentation of the Harlem Renaissance. He was awarded the Metropolitan Museum of Art Life Fellowship Award in 1970, the President's Living Legacy Award in 1978, and an honorary doctorate from Howard University in 1983, the year he died. Since then, his work has been the subject of major art exhibitions and is still considered required viewing for anyone who wants to learn about the lives and achievements of the people of that historic era in Harlem.

Laura Wheeler Waring

Painter
1887–1948

Some have called Laura Wheeler Waring a traditionalist, as if that diminished her contribution to the Harlem Renaissance. They point out that the appeal of her work belonged more to the black middle class than to the working class. However, while she painted in the accepted European styles, Laura used her brushes and canvas to make strong, truthful statements on America's race issues.

Laura was born in Hartford, Connecticut, in 1887. In 1914,

she won the Cresson Foreign Traveling Scholarship, which allowed her to study in Europe and North Africa. She continued her studies at the Pennsylvania Academy of Fine Arts from 1918 to 1924, returning to Paris, France, for one year to study at the Académie de la Grande Chaumiére. Waring learned all she could in Rome, Italy, and Paris. She even studied under the world-famous sculptor Auguste Rodin. Then she returned to pass on her knowledge to generations of artists at Cheyney State Teacher's College (now Cheyney University) near Philadelphia, Pennsylvania.

Waring's portraits are known for the genuine warmth and affection with which she painted African-Americans. Much like May Howard Jackson, Waring had a humanistic approach to painting. At a time when it was openly denied that blacks were human on the same level as whites, Laura Waring focused on that very humanity, capturing it on canvas for all to see.

Waring made sure to indicate the social background of the people she painted. Often they were well-to-do mulattoes shown in comfortable surroundings, as if to say, "See, we Negroes are not so different after all. We live and feel and hope just like any other American."

Showing that African-Americans were capable of mastering the fine arts was considered a very important achievement. Many believed it would prove that African-Americans had achieved a level of culture equal to the best the white world could offer. That, in part, is why many sought to excel in traditional painting styles. But even within the traditional, Waring found ways to be daring. Her intimate style invited the viewer to see more than just the moment captured on the canvas. She made people think about what that person's life must be like: where they lived, what kind of lifestyle they led, as well as what they might be thinking at the moment shown in the painting.

Waring portrayed black Americans as people who were poised, gentle, and fully aware of the difficulties they faced, no matter what their social or financial status. She won the Harmon Foundation gold medal for her portrait of Anna Washington Derry in 1927.

The painting skillfully records the years and the trials of that gentle lady in her posture and care-worn gaze. Her hands, which once held laughing children and baked fresh bread, now are crossed upon her small, frail chest. She has nothing left to hold but herself. Her eyes seem to look back across the years, sifting through memories both happy and sad. It is a portrait of a proud but tired woman whose only piece of jewelry was her plain gold wedding band. Laura had painted a moving but rarely portrayed image of black womanhood.

Waring could be daring too. Her portrait of a mother and daughter created quite a stir because it focused attention on the mixing of the races. May Howard Jackson had been the first to question the nation's forced segregation—the separation of black and white people—when in reality the races had mixed more than anyone cared to admit. Laura demonstrated in painting what May Jackson showed in sculpture.

Waring's *Mother and Daughter* features two young women in profile. They are so similar in looks that they could be mistaken for sisters. Yet it is clear to see that the mother, in the background, is mulatto while her daughter, several shades lighter in skin color and more Caucasian in her features, could be classified as quadroon. The serene expressions of the mother and daughter give no indication of just how controversial the painting was at the time.

Anything that showed blending of the races was thought to be taboo and was avoided by most artists. May Jackson and Laura Waring were two pioneering African-American women. Each woman was considered "traditional" in her own artistic style. Yet both women radically expanded the kinds of images that could represent black Americans.

These examples only go to prove that labels such as traditionalist, modernist, realist, and others need not limit an artist's power to make statements that would appear to lie outside their area. We can all find ways to work outside the labels that others put on us.

Waring remained at her beloved Cheyney State Teacher's College throughout her professional career. She was an instructor from 1906 to 1925 and from 1925 until her death in 1948 she was the director of both the art and music departments. No other black female painter achieved the national recognition that Laura Waring enjoyed during the Harlem Renaissance. Not only did she win awards and exhibit widely, but she worked tirelessly to pass on her wisdom and experience through teaching. The Harmon Foundation also welcomed her training and experience on the occasions that she joined the panel of judges for their exhibitions. Laura Wheeler Waring was one of the few artists capable of turning stale tradition into extraordinary expression.

William Henry Johnson

Painter
1901–1970

*I*t was such a struggle simply to become an art-ist that many were unable to shake off the outmoded model of the academy and the false sense of achievement that the academy repre-sented. In their prolonged sacrifices and the hard work . . . it took to achieve schooling and recognition they inevitably were driven toward the academic standards to end their uncertainties, to prove they were artists.

—Romare Bearden and
Harry Henderson,
A History of African-American
Artists: From 1792 to the Present

At a time when some black artists were praised for their lack of formal art instruction, William Henry Johnson labored to get a superb art education, including training throughout Europe. In the end, his greatest satisfaction and greatest works came from portraying his own people going about their lives with quiet dignity.

His simplified, heartfelt expression was a result of his years of difficult study and great personal sacrifice. Yet he was often criticized for the very thing that led him to his deeply personal style—his education, and his European experience with the strange new art form called modernism.

William was born on March 18, 1901, in the small town of Florence, South Carolina. His mother was of black and Sioux Indian ancestry. His father was reported to be a wealthy white man, well known in Florence, who completely deserted his son.

His mother later married a black man and had four other children—two boys and two girls. When an accident crippled his stepfather, William's mother supported the family by working for white people. She washed, ironed, cooked—whatever was needed.

William taught himself to draw by copying comics in the newspaper. He was determined to become an artist. He heard that the art center of America was in New York City, but he had no way to get there.

Johnson's answer came when he learned that his uncle was going to New York for the high wages paid for wartime jobs in the city. Johnson convinced his mother to let him go along. He and his uncle journeyed to New York in 1918, when Johnson was seventeen years old.

They took jobs as stevedores, dockworkers who loaded supplies onto ships. Johnson also took odd jobs. He worked both day and night so that he could send money home to his mother and still save up enough to pay for art training.

Johnson knew that because he was black, his paintings would have to be better than just "good." They would have to be of the highest quality, beyond reproach, so that no one could deny his accomplishments. The school he chose for his training was the National Academy of Design, which offered the most demanding academic training available for artists.

Johnson advanced quickly, mastering skills and winning prizes in student competitions. His work was soon noted by Charles Webster Hawthorne, a painter with an impressive reputation as one of America's most inspiring teachers. He strongly believed that an artist should show people his or her own way of seeing life—the artist's individual vision. "The painter . . . must show people more than they already see," he said. "Here is where art comes in." Johnson remembered those words

At the National Academy of Design, Johnson won the Canon Prize in 1924 and 1926. He won the Hallgarten Prize in 1925. He went on to win five other prizes, but there was one that he failed to win—the one he wanted most of all—a one-year study trip to Europe.

Charles Hawthorne and several other academy artists felt that prejudice was the reason Johnson was not awarded the European study prize. They refused to accept that he would be denied the chance to study in the great art centers of Europe.

Hawthorne had enlisted the radical artist George Luks to assist in Johnson's art training. Luks was part of an artists' group known as "the Eight." They believed that paintings should show true realism. George Luks was known for portraying the spiritual strength of working-class people. He taught Johnson, and in return, Johnson cleaned Luks's brushes and studio. Between Hawthorne and Luks, enough money was raised to send Johnson to Europe to study for a year. He arrived in Paris, France, in November 1926.

Paris was like nothing Johnson had ever seen or could have imagined. He was free of the constant restraints of American segregation, and was thrilled by European artists' rapidly changing styles. At the time his favorite artist was Paul Gauguin.

Gauguin believed that machines were dominating society and killing creativity. He left a comfortable banker's life to live with the so-called primitive natives of Tahiti. Gauguin felt strongly that the Tahitian way of life was more natural, though like most Europeans he still used the degrading word "primitive" when he spoke of the brown-skinned, native people. He then declared that he, too, was a primitive.

Johnson promptly declared himself a "primitive" also. For Johnson, to be "primitive" meant he was a sensitive man who lived outside a so called civilized society that hated him because of the color of his skin. Johnson saw in Gauguin a modern master artist who painted the honest and spiritual quality of people of color.

Johnson did not try to paint like Gauguin, though. He searched, instead, for a style that could express the storm of emotions he felt inside. William found it in the example of the French painter Chaim Soutine.

In all his years of study, working to gain more control and discipline over the paint and brushes, Johnson finally found a way to free himself from those narrow limitations. This style, new even in Europe, let Johnson release his conflicting emotions onto the canvas. The results were very strange to see, but had a strong ring of truth. So Johnson borrowed from the style of Soutine, but he changed it and turned it into his own personal expression.

In 1929, Johnson returned to America determined to make a name for himself in the arts. He entered six paintings in the upcoming Harmon Exhibition. He won the Harmon gold medal and first prize of $400. Four of his paintings were also selected to be part of the Harmon traveling exhibition that toured cities nationwide.

An excited Johnson took many paintings home to Florence, South Carolina, to show his mother. An exhibition of his paintings was held at the

YMCA, and he was reported on in the local news. But a few days later he was arrested while painting an image of the Jacobia Hotel, a notorious brothel. It is unknown if he was arrested because what he was painting was an embarrassment to many people in the town or because some were angry about his national fame—something Negroes were not supposed to have. In any case, Johnson was very angry about the unjust jailing in his own hometown. He left Florence and did not return again for fourteen years.

Johnson married Holcha Krake in 1930. She was a white artist from Denmark who wove tapestries and was a skilled ceramist (an artist who makes objects from clay and bakes them in very high heat until they harden). They had met in 1929 and even though she was fifteen years older, they fell in love. They moved to Kerteminde, her hometown in Denmark, a small fishing village where they could live cheaply.

In the early 1930s, they bicycled and camped through Sweden, Norway, Germany, and North Africa, but the deepening world depression and rise of Adolf Hitler and his Nazis in Germany told Johnson that it was time to leave Europe. Johnson had already felt deep disappointment that after ten years in Europe, the great success he wished for still eluded him.

He also felt that he needed to reconnect with his own people and their lives in the United States. With the threat of Hitler and his lethal campaign against modern art and what he called the degenerate races—Jews and Negroes—Johnson felt doubly threatened. He and Holcha came to the United States in November 1938.

Holcha was amazed by the hostility of American whites to their interracial marriage. They had not encountered such treatment in Europe. But now, despite Johnson's excellent training and long experience in Europe, he could neither find a job nor sell his paintings. This deeply frustrated Johnson who saw that two other black American painters, Horace Pippin and Jacob Lawrence, had achieved the kind of recognition for which he longed.

Young Pastry Cook, *by William Henry Johnson*

Inspired by the two young painters, Johnson began evolving his style. For subject matter, he turned to the biblical stories and spiritual songs he had heard as a child back in Florence, South Carolina.

Johnson's new paintings were even more simplified than his previous works. His conversations with the legendary Henry Ossawa Tanner while in Europe had given him a deeper understanding of the powerful role of religion in African-American history. A new sense of calm and peace was evident in the newer paintings.

In the biblical paintings, Johnson portrayed a black Christ as a serene symbol of hope. He followed these works with paintings of common folk: street musicians, lindy-hoppers, churchgoing scenes, farm scenes, and even portraits. In all of these paintings, William painted African-Americans as calm and dignified, but also with a feeling of warm, familiar friendliness.

He used a printing technique called silk screen, which he learned while working in the government's Works Progress Administration, to make multiple prints of some of his paintings. These were more affordable for average folk than his original paintings.

In 1942, Johnson was given a "Certificate of Honor for distinguished service to America in art." But in 1944 his wife, Holcha, died of breast cancer. Johnson was never the same after that. What his friends did not know was that he was also suffering from a severe mental illness that was slowly affecting both his mind and his skills.

Johnson sacrificed and saved to pay for a trip to Denmark in hopes of marrying his dead wife's sister, but when he arrived, she turned down his proposal. Six months later he went to Oslo, the capital city of Norway, intending to exhibit his paintings there. On that trip, he was found wandering the streets, delirious. Johnson was returned to New York and spent the next twenty-three years in a New York state mental hospital. He died on April 13, 1970.

Were it not for the Harmon Foundation and its director, Mary Beattie Brady, the life's work of William Henry Johnson would have been lost to us. Mary Brady rescued more than a thousand works from being thrown away by the storage company that held them—the storage fees had not been paid for years. Johnson's wonderful contribution to American art—his ultramodern approach—was sometimes humorous. But it always expressed the essential dignity and humanity of African-Americans and added greatly to the diverse images of the New Negro.

Archibald Motley Jr.

Painter
1891–1981

In my painting I have tried to paint the Negro as I have seen him and as I feel him, in myself without adding or detracting, just being frankly honest.

With this attitude, Archibald Motley Jr. became the first artist of any race to consider the social life of African-Americans in the bustling northern cities as worthy subjects of art.

Archibald Motley Jr. was born on October 7, 1891, in New Orleans, Louisiana. The family did not stay there long, however. Archibald's father had a general merchandise store, but threats from his white competitors drove him out of business, and out of town. The family finally settled in Chicago where Mr. Motley became a Pullman porter.

Archibald was always drawing something. His school notebooks were filled with his sketches. While in high school, he once told his father to give up any ideas of him ever becoming a doctor. Archibald was convinced that he could be nothing except an artist. His father had other ideas. He suggested that Archibald take up architecture as a more practical career. But Archibald was determined to go his own way. He told his father, "I want to do something completely out of my soul, out of my mind."

Before the start of World War I, Motley enrolled in the Art Institute of Chicago. He earned enough to pay tuition with jobs such as dusting statuary and moving chairs and easels. This work, along with other odd jobs and twenty-five cents a day from his father, allowed him to complete four years of study.

At the Art Institute of Chicago, Motley did not experience the same kinds of racial prejudice suffered by black artists in other parts of the country. Later in his career, he stated that he was treated with "great respect" by both faculty and students while attending classes at the institute.

But what Motley remembered most was the class taught by George Walcott on the use of color to plan a painting. Walcott taught Motley how to draw a grid of rectangles on his canvas as guides to painting large, colored abstract shapes. He would then fill in around these areas with smaller areas of colored shapes to create a soothing play of lighter and darker, brighter and duller areas. Only then would Motley paint the colors and shapes as people and things. It was a lot of work, but the end result was a painting that seemed to suggest that there was something wonderful and magical going on in the lives of the people he painted.

Motley graduated from the Chicago Institute of Art, but he was turned down each time he applied for a commercial art job. To support himself he worked as a plumber, coal shoveler, laborer—anything he could find. He was very much afraid of failure, and this kept him from entering his paintings in the annual institute exhibits. He later recalled, "In school, you always depend upon that instructor to straighten you out. . . . When you are alone, a lot of people lose their confidence. I lost a lot of confidence."

In 1925, with several years of positive reactions to his paintings to bolster his confidence, the quiet dignity of his grandmother in his painting *Mending Socks* was very well received. His portrait of a doctor's wife titled *A Mulatress* (a term that identified the genteel woman's mixed racial heritage) won the $200 Frank G. Logan Prize.

Motley entered a third painting that he had been advised not to submit because it was a dance hall scene. Many middle-class people of that time felt that certain subjects should not be portrayed in the "high arts" because they were "low-life" scenes. Scenes of working-class people, the poor, bars, brothels, and the carefree atmosphere of interracial jazz clubs all fell into the "low-life" group.

Motley felt, however, that the painting of nightlife on crowded city streets eerily lit by glowing streetlights belonged in the exhibition. So he entered a painting called *Syncopation,* against the advice of his friends. That painting won the $200 Joseph Eisendrath Award and was highly praised by critics. Motley then entered the painting *Black Belt,* another scene of black Americans and city nightlife, for the 1928 Harmon exhibition. It won the gold medal and paved the way for a one-man show in New York City. Edward Alden Jewell, an art critic for the *New York Times,* decided to devote a major article to Motley and his one-man show. Edward Jewell was highly respected as one of America's leading art critics. Jewell's review of Motley's work resulted in twenty-two of twenty-six paintings in the show being sold. Motley made between $6,000 and $7,000 from that exhibition. Finally, at the age of thirty-seven and after years of part-time jobs, Motley could support himself entirely with his art.

Some black leaders continued to criticize Motley's paintings of gambling, dancing, and the "sportin' life" as contributing to the negative stereotypes of blacks. Others see people rushing, moving, trying to get someplace better in Motley's rich glowing colors and scenes. They would say that Motley's scenes represented African-Americans with a sense of self-respect, honesty, and dignity in their daily lives.

In 1929, Motley won a Guggenheim Fellowship to study in Europe for a year. Of all the black American artists who went to Europe during the Harlem Renaissance, Motley was the only one who made no effort to meet and talk with the legendary Henry Ossawa Tanner. Motley isolated himself from his fellow Americans and never met the others who were also studying in Europe, such as Augusta Savage, Hale Woodruff, William H. Johnson, and Palmer Hayden. He said he ignored their invitations because, "when you go to a foreign country, you don't go there to see Americans."

Motley and his wife returned from Europe as the Great Depression was beginning in America. While many other artists, black and white, were having a very difficult time in the depressed economy of the 1930s, Motley found steady work in the first federal arts program, the Public Works of Art Project. He was later made a supervisor on the Works Progress Administration art project. This steady work carried him until the WPA art programs were phased out in 1940.

Because he was still the most famous black artist working in Chicago, there remained a demand for his paintings and he worked steadily until 1945. That year his wife died, leaving him severely depressed and unable to paint. He did not return to painting again until 1953. He died in 1981.

Archibald Motley Jr. devoted his artistic career to portraying the spirit and optimism of black urban life. He did not waver from his vision of the beauty of the nightlife of the cities even in the face of pressure and criticism. Today, he stands as the first artist to show that the social lives of African-Americans in the North were worthy subjects of fine art. In doing so, he expressed much of the mood and feeling behind the New Negro movement—progress, hope, and self-respect.

Richmond Barthé

Sculptor
1901–1989

*R*ichmond Barthé has come to us at a time when we are sadly in need of real inspiration—of that spiritual food that heartens and strengthens . . . hopes that embody the willingness to do the larger and truer things in life.

—William H. A. Moore in *Opportunity*, November 1928

As a sculptor, Richmond Barthé found a middle ground between academic tradition and realistic, emotionally moving studies of Africans and black Americans. Barthé often portrayed blacks as individuals with grace, strength, and an inspiring sense of quiet dignity. Some have even said that his portrayals defined, in visual form, the New Negro.

Richmond Barthé was born on January 28, 1901, in Bay St. Louis on the Mississippi Gulf Coast. His father, Richmond Barthé Sr., died when Richmond was only a few months old. His mother, Marie Clementine Robateau, was a descendant of free blacks from St. Martinsville, Louisiana. For six years after his father's death, she supported the family as a seamstress. She later married Richmond's godfather, William Franklin, a workingman and musician.

As a child, Richmond remembered that "my mother gave me paper and pencil to play with. . . . It kept me quiet while she did her errands . . . My mother and I would give names to the people I drew and make up stories about them."

Young Richmond used to help his stepfather deliver ice in the summertime. A wealthy woman from New Orleans took a liking to Richmond and worried that carrying the ice on his shoulders would give him rheumatism. She sent Richmond to a friend of hers, Mrs. Pond, with a letter asking her to give Richmond a job. Mrs. Pond took Richmond with her to New Orleans and from then, until the age of twenty-three, Richmond worked for the wealthy Pond family.

It seems strange to us that such a young boy would leave his family to work in a stranger's house miles from his home, but work was very hard to find in those days, especially for African-Americans. Working for a wealthy and prestigious family could give a black child a better chance in life.

Richmond dreamed that one day he would leave the Ponds and become an artist. The Reverend Jack Kane, pastor of the Catholic Blessed Sacrament

Church, saw a painting that Richmond had done for a church festival and was very impressed by it. He soon discovered, though, that Richmond had no funds to pay for art school, and further, that none of the local art schools would take black students.

Father Kane put up his own money so that Barthé could attend an art school up north—the School of the Art Institute of Chicago. Barthé took a job as a waiter in a French restaurant to help support himself while studying at the institute from 1924 to 1928. During that time, he concentrated on painting, anatomy, and figure construction.

It was during his final year of school that Barthé's favorite teacher, the renowned painter Charles Schroeder, told him to model some heads in clay. Schroeder explained that the exercise would help Barthé's painting by giving him a better feel for the third dimension. Barthé recalled:

> *I did heads of two classmates, one male and one female. They turned out so well, I cast them and they were shown during "the Negro in Art Week." The critics praised them and I was asked to do busts of Henry Ossawa Tanner and Toussaint L'Overture for the Lake County Children's Home in Gary, Indiana.*

Barthé showed photographs of these pieces and some others he had done to Jo Davidson and Lorado Taft, who were very respected sculptors. They said that Barthé should avoid further instruction in sculpting because his sculptures had a spiritual quality that he might lose if influenced too much by an instructor. Because Barthé already knew anatomy, he did not need any help with the proportions. From then on, Richmond Barthé would be a sculptor, and it was that unspoiled "spiritual" quality that made Barthé's sculptures so popular.

In 1929, Barthé left Chicago to study in New York at the Art Students

League. He won an honorable mention in the 1929 Harmon exhibition. He then returned briefly to Chicago in 1930 and won a Julius Rosenwald Fund Fellowship.

Barthé returned to New York in 1931 and got an amazing career break. He was given a one-man show at the prestigious D'Caz-Delbo Gallery. At that time, the influential, white-owned New York galleries rarely included the art of blacks in their exhibits. For Barthé, a young black artist early in his career, to receive a coveted one-man show from such a gallery was truly remarkable.

The exhibition received high praise from art critics: "a sculptor of unmistakable promise . . . [his] modeling is most sensitive, communicating . . . the spirit of the subject. . . . Richmond Barthé penetrates far beneath the surface, honestly seeking essentials, and never . . . superficial allure. . . . Some of the readings deserve, indeed, to be called profound."

Barthé's success in New York brought him to the attention of Gertrude V. Whitney, the director of the Whitney Museum of American Art. She organized an exhibition of his sculpture, and the museum bought three of his works, *Blackberry Woman, African Dancer,* and *The Comedian.*

The recognition he was receiving prompted other museums and art collectors to pay attention to Barthé's work. Because of this success he was able to afford to go to Europe to tour the museums and galleries there, which led to more exhibitions and critical acclaim overseas.

During the Great Depression of the 1930s, the attitudes that had sustained the Harlem Renaissance and the nation's interest in its black citizens vanished. Still, Barthé enjoyed the fruits of critical acclaim. In 1937, he received a commission by the federal Public Works of Art Project to create two massive panels, each 8 by 40 feet long, for the Harlem River Housing Project amphitheater. The panels were titled *Dance* and *Exodus.*

The Blackberry Woman, *by Richmond Barthé*

In March 1939, Barthé had his largest exhibition ever. It included eighteen bronze statues and was held at the Arden Galleries in New York City. That show paved the way for him to receive the coveted Guggenheim Fellowship in 1940 and 1941.

In 1941, the United States entered World War II, and Barthé became the most publicized black artist in the country. America needed visible examples to show black citizens, white citizens, and our allies in the war that despite forced separation of the races and racial discrimination America was, somehow, still democratic. Barthé was asked to participate in numerous political and social functions to give the impression that America was giving her black citizens a fair opportunity to succeed. This was, of course, not true, but for the leaders of the nation it was more important that it appeared to be true than for it to actually be true. Later in his life, Barthé looked back on those days. He said that it was meant to be "the answer to Hitler and the Japanese who said that 'America talks democracy, but look at the American Negro'. . . . I think I have gotten more publicity than most white artists, much of it because I was a Negro."

Unfortunately, the publicity did not add up to art sales. While Barthé was shown off as an example of American fairness and democracy, he was barely able to support himself. Artistic trends were also changing rapidly. Modern art was on the rise worldwide, making Barthé's more traditional sculptures seem outdated by comparison.

Barthé continued to work in the style that had meaning and purpose for him, however. He never experimented with abstractions (exaggerating familiar forms until they no longer look familiar, or even recognizable), mythology, or symbolism. He died on March 5, 1989, in Pasadena, California.

Throughout his career, Richmond Barthé portrayed the spirit of people of African ancestry in a way that had not been seen in America before. He remained true to that vision all his life, never changing his style to suit passing trends. Though he did not shy away from portraying the passions, hardships, and cruelties experienced by African-Americans, his sculptures stand as songs of praise about the grace, beauty, and dignity of people of African descent everywhere in the world.

Hale Aspacio Woodruff

Painter and Educator
1900–1980

This was supposedly Klan country! Yet here they were giving me $150 along with praise. Knowing the history and reality of the way we were treated day in and day out, it was virtually unbelievable!

—Hale Woodruff's reaction upon receiving an invitation to exhibit and have supper with the women of a ladies' literary club in Franklin, Indiana

As an artist and an educator, Hale Aspacio Woodruff was

constantly in search of ways to bring art into the everyday lives of African-Americans. He wanted to surround black people with their own proud history. He taught generations of young black artists to look honestly at their surroundings as an important source of identity and purpose.

Hale was born in Cairo, Illinois, on August 26, 1900. George Woodruff, his father, died shortly after his birth, and his mother, Augusta Bell Woodruff, moved to Nashville and took up domestic work. She taught Hale how to draw, hoping it would keep him occupied when she had to leave him alone for long hours while she worked. Hale learned quickly and was soon copying comics out of the newspaper or engravings from the family Bible. While at Pearl High School, Hale was the cartoonist for the school paper. He was certain that he would become an artist.

Woodruff attended the John Herron Art Institute in Indianapolis, Indiana. In exchange for working as a desk clerk, he was given a room at the "colored" YMCA. He earned $5 per week by drawing a political cartoon for a local black newspaper. The owner of an art-supply store, a German named Herman Lieber, gave Woodruff a book on African sculpture. Woodruff was amazed by what he saw. He was unaware of the significance of African art and was amazed to see it photographed so beautifully and treated as a serious topic of study.

Although he did very well in his studies, he was eventually no longer able to pay the tuition and had to leave the Herron Institute. Woodruff heard of an upcoming exhibition by the Harmon Foundation. In 1926, he painted a large canvas of two dignified elderly black women. The piece won second prize, the Harmon bronze medal, and $100.

Mary Brady, director of the Harmon Foundation, contacted local newspapers saying that an unknown local artist had won an important national contest. Not only did the press report on it, but the governor called

Woodruff and asked for "the honor" of coming to the YMCA and presenting the medal personally.

A nearby ladies' literary club in Franklin, Indiana, invited Hale to exhibit his paintings and have supper with them. He was simply amazed that, in what he considered to be "Ku Klux Klan country," a ladies' club was offering him dinner, praise, and $150. With these and other commissions and awards and the sales of his paintings, Woodruff bought a third-class ticket and headed for Paris, France. While there, he met two legends of the art world—Henry Ossawa Tanner and Alain Locke.

Woodruff spent an extraordinary rainy afternoon discussing art and art history with Tanner. He truly felt that Tanner accepted him as an artist. That the internationally famous Tanner would share views and technical painting problems with him was a tremendous source of encouragement for Woodruff.

Alain Locke, a respected professor of philosophy at Howard University and a leading African-American collector of African art, took Woodruff to a flea market, where Woodruff was able to purchase a finely carved Bembe ancestral figure from the Congo for $2. Hale Woodruff's extensive collection of African sculpture began with that one small piece.

Woodruff returned from France in 1931, after four years of study abroad. John Hope, president of the recently formed Atlanta University, offered him a teaching position. When Woodruff accepted, he became the first African-American artist with advanced training and European experience to teach art in a southern black university.

Woodruff looked for ways to make art a larger part of the lives of his students and their families. He started a printmaking program so that the students could put their works of art into the hands and homes of relatives and friends. He wanted to make art more accessible and more meaningful to everyone—not just the students in his classes. Woodruff had a vision of community involvement in the arts.

He went to the High Museum of Art in Atlanta and got special permission to take his students there to view their art collection. No black had ever entered the museum unless they worked there—the museum simply did not welcome blacks. Because of Hale Woodruff, blacks gained access into this "white-only" institution long before the civil rights movements of the 1960s.

Woodruff taught his students to paint their surroundings and to document the land and lives that they lived with a sense of honesty, identity, and purpose. But Woodruff was still in search of a larger, bolder means to bring art to the community. Woodruff found his answer in the example of Diego Rivera and the other Mexican muralists. Their huge murals—paintings on walls—told the people of Mexico's valiant struggles and history.

Woodruff traveled to Mexico in the summer of 1936 where he encountered very harsh prejudice against black Americans. He studied the Mexican muralists' techniques so that he could bring the essence of that art form home to black America. Woodruff returned to find that Talladega College in Alabama had exactly the kind of project he was looking for. They wanted a series of murals about the *Amistad* mutiny to instill pride and show the students that Africans did not go meekly into slavery.

The *Amistad* was a Spanish slave ship. An African prince, Cinque, led the slaves on board. They revolted, killed some of the crew, and took over the ship. They were later captured and tried for mutiny and murder. Former president John Quincy Adams came out of retirement to defend the right of these men to defend themselves against slavery. Adams won the case and the Africans were allowed to return to their homeland.

Woodruff spent many hours researching the smallest details and searching for portraits of each of the people present in the courtroom so his painting of them would be historically accurate. This contribution to American art was entirely unique.

Aaron Douglas had painted the *Aspects of Negro Life,* a history of the African-American from Africa through the rural South to the industrial centers of the North. But Douglas's historical piece was more symbolic than literal. Woodruff had created a historically accurate painting of African-American history to educate and to inspire.

Woodruff would paint more murals of African-American history, including *The Art of the Negro* for Atlanta University in 1950. Woodruff retired from teaching in 1968 and was still actively painting when he died in 1980 at the age of eighty. Hale Aspacio Woodruff, an educator and artist, brought the rich lessons of history to students and public alike. Some, such as the ladies' literary society of Franklin, Indiana, surprised him with their genuine interest and good wishes. Woodruff's murals still stand as both education and inspiration. They were made possible by his exacting research and masterful brushstrokes.

Palmer C. Hayden

Painter
1890–1973

I paint what us Negroes, colored people, us Americans know. We're a brand-new race, raised and manufactured in the United States. I do like to paint what they did.

Palmer Hayden was determined to paint the scenes of everyday black life in an honest and clear way. His paintings combine his imagination with his rich life experiences as an artist, laborer, army cavalryman, and circus roustabout. (A roustabout was a worker who

helped set up the tents, games of chance, and brightly painted circus exhibits.) Palmer supported himself with hard physical labor for much of his youth, which gave him a great respect and admiration for working-class people. While some artists believed only in painting beautiful things for rich society people, Palmer painted the humor, tragedy and comforts of a working-class, black lifestyle.

Palmer Hayden was born Peyton Cole Hedgeman on January 15, 1890, in Widewater, Virginia. His father, James Hedgeman, was a slave who had been freed by the Civil War. Peyton's mother, Nancy Belle Cole, was related to the Moncures, one of the leading families of Virginia. It is said that the Moncures recognized their kinship with her "in their own way."

The Hedgemans had ten children, and Peyton was number five. His mother laughed at the "pot-bellied" cows he drew on his school tablet, but to Peyton, anything that got his busy mother's attention was important.

At the age of seventeen, Peyton left home to make a life for himself, just as his older brothers and sisters had done. In Washington, D.C., he tried to find a job as an assistant to a commercial artist so he could learn the trade. But none of the white commercial artists would hire him. Eventually, in an adventurous mood, Peyton joined the Ringling Brothers Circus and traveled with it all over the country. The best part was that he was free to draw after the tents were set up. He made good money painting portraits of the circus performers.

Finding steady work was hard for a black man back then, so in 1911 Peyton remembered his mother's advice and joined the U.S. Army. His mother had once told him that at least in the army he would have a place to eat and sleep. The army recruiter told Peyton that he needed a letter of reference—something that was only required of black Americans. The man he asked to write the letter was very annoyed and wrote down Palmer C. Hayden instead of Peyton C. Hedgeman. The army enlisted him under that name and from then on he was known as Palmer C. Hayden. When Hayden was discharged in 1920, he was more determined than ever to become a professional artist.

He took a night-shift job at the post office so that he could attend a six-week course in painting and drawing at Columbia University in New York. He moved to Greenwich Village, in New York City, to be around other artists.

Hayden became close friends with the artist Cloyd Boykin who was also from Virginia. Boykin, like Hayden, had to work to support himself while he studied to improve his painting skills. Boykin worked as a janitor. One of Hayden's most famous paintings was his portrayal of Boykin titled *The Janitor Who Paints.* Hayden later said, "I painted it because no one called Boykin 'the artist.' They called him 'the janitor.'"

By offering to work in return for instruction, Hayden was admitted to a summer art colony run by Asa E. Randall at Boothbay Harbor, Maine. He learned so much about color and layout relationships that he considered his time there a "real turning point" in his artistic education.

While returning home from a part-time job as a window washer, Hayden met a black man on the street who needed help moving furniture for an elderly white lady. After several hours of work, the man had to leave, and Hayden finished the job alone. The woman asked Hayden to return once or twice a week to clean and dust her apartment. On one of those visits, she learned of his desire to be a painter.

One day the woman showed Hayden a flier for the first Harmon competition, the William E. Harmon Awards for Distinguished Achievement among Negroes. Hayden entered one of his paintings of Boothbay Harbor and won the $400 first prize.

Because he was an unknown artist from the South, he received a lot of newspaper attention. Although some said that Hayden's paintings were not as good as the more highly trained painters in the competition, the critics said that his work symbolized the arrival in the North of talented black artists from the South, overcoming many hardships along the way.

When she heard of Hayden's accomplishment, the lady gave him $3,000 to study art in Paris saying, "Now you've made something to talk about. Now's the time you should go abroad." Hayden, honoring her wish, never revealed the name of the woman who had told him of the 1926 Harmon Foundation competition.

He left for Paris in March 1927. While there he met Laura Wheeler Waring who suggested that he visit Henry Ossawa Tanner. Tanner knew of Hayden's Harmon prize and welcomed Hayden into his studio. Hayden often visited the old master painter and received many tips from him, though not all were art related. Tanner advised Hayden on French people's attitudes and customs, and how to get along with them. "Tanner never said anything discouraging to you," Hayden later remembered. Hayden also met Alain Locke who was traveling through Paris en route to Africa on one of his many art-collecting trips. Though Hayden did not feel that African art held much meaning for African-Americans, he was inspired to create the painting *Fétiche et Fleurs*.

In that painting, Hayden included a piece of African sculpture and a specially woven African cloth. *Fétiche et Fleurs* received much recognition for the use of African objects in what had been a traditionally European kind of painting.

Although Hayden could appreciate African art, he did not take to modern art—cubism and abstractions. His passion was to tell stories with his paintings and he did not feel modern art would help him to do that.

Hayden studied in Paris for five years, returning to America in 1932. He had supported himself in part by sending back paintings to Mary Beattie Brady at the Harmon Foundation, who sold them. Though he had learned a great deal from the different schools, museums, and artists, Hayden felt that the greatest gift of studying in Paris was the freedom of living without the racial limitations of America. It greatly increased his self-confidence.

Upon his return to New York, Mary Brady gave Hayden a job at the Harmon Foundation, helping to prepare the traveling exhibitions of black artists. In his own paintings, Hayden remained a storyteller.

Many of his works were misunderstood. He was criticized for not showing African-Americans as well dressed and in upper-class surroundings, but the criticism never bothered him. Hayden was only interested in painting what was important to him. He portrayed the humor, tragedy, and lifestyle of blacks who, like himself, had come north hoping to find a better life in the cities. His most famous work came after the Renaissance—the *John Henry* series. In it, Hayden told the true story of that "steel-driving man," and established himself as the nation's leading painter of black folklore. Palmer C. Hayden continued painting until his death in 1973 at the Veterans Administration Hospital in Manhattan.

Hayden's paintings are unique because he did more than simply imitate on canvas what was happening around him. He felt driven to interpret what he saw and loved in African-American life—its humor as well as its beauty.

Horace Pippin

Painter
1888–1946

orace Pippin explored many different areas of African-American life as well as the universal human yearning for peace. A deeply spiritual man, he searched continually in his paintings for peace, for the sense of home that he knew as a child.

It has been said that Horace Pippin "belongs to those naive painters who are devoted to fact as a thing to be known and respected, but not necessarily imitated." He worked more at getting the feeling of a scene than at trying to make his painting look exactly like the scene. He was born on February 22, 1888, in West Chester, Pennsylvania, a suburb of Philadelphia. He did not know his father. His mother moved to Goshen, New York, to be near her relatives and to find domestic work.

Horace loved to draw; he just could not seem to stop himself. In school, he would draw on his assignments, and it got him into a lot of trouble. He later recalled, "If the word was dog, stove, dishpan, or something like that, I had a sketch of the article at the end of the work. And the results were, I would have to stay in after school and finish my lesson the right way. The worse part was, I would get a beating when I got home for coming home late, regardless of what I were kept in for."

Horace was deeply affected by his life in Goshen and all the things he saw there—the "orderliness" and rituals of life there, the Saturday-night bath, the seasonal farmwork, the interracial harmony of women gathering daily at the milkman's wagon, and the town's reliance on biblical values. These themes appeared in Horace's work throughout his artistic life.

Horace helped his mother by hiring himself out for odd jobs. One day, when he was fourteen, Horace was working at a farm owned by James Gaven. Mr. Gaven was so tired that he fell asleep after supper, right at the dinner table. Horace sketched Mr. Gaven while he slept. After he woke up, Mr. Gaven saw the sketch that Horace had done and wanted to send Horace to an art school. But Horace's mother's illness forced him to work to support her.

Horace took all sorts of jobs to earn money—cutting wood, clearing fields, unloading coal. At eighteen, he got a job as a porter at the St. Elmo Hotel, where he worked for seven years. His mother died in 1911. The following year he left Goshen and moved to Paterson, New Jersey.

Pippin volunteered for military service when the United States entered World War I in 1917. He was proud to serve and proud to be promoted to corporal before his unit left Fort Dix. At the time, white American soldiers refused to fight beside blacks. Pippin's unit was transferred to a French command as the historic 369th Infantry. The 369th was an all-volunteer black regiment, except for its white officers. Pippin was a squad leader in that most highly decorated American unit. They alone received France's highest honor for valor in service, the famed Croix de Guerre.

Corporal Pippin was shot in the shoulder in 1918. The bullet destroyed nerves, muscle, and bone, and it crippled his right arm. He spent five months in army hospitals before he was discharged on May 22, 1919. His right hand had to be tied to his body. When the 369th, also called the Harlem Hellfighters, marched up New York City's Fifth Avenue and through Harlem in their triumphant victory parade, Pippin's injury prevented him from participating. He quietly returned to West Chester, Pennsylvania, where his mother's family lived. It was very hard for a man like Pippin, who had worked and made his own way all his life, to scrape by on his tiny soldier's pension.

Pippin met Jennie Ora Featherstone shortly after arriving in West Chester. On November 21, 1920, they were married. Jennie was a widow with a young son, and now Pippin had a family that could not be supported on his army pension alone. Jennie took in washing to help make ends meet. Pippin helped by picking up and delivering the laundry in a small wagon.

Times were difficult for black Americans following World War I, but there was also great optimism. The number of white men fighting in the war left many job opportunities in the northern cities for African-Americans who would normally not have been considered for such work. Advancements in many fields of endeavor by black Americans such as Henry Ossawa Tanner, Paul Laurence Dunbar, Booker T. Washington, Paul Robeson, and Frederick Douglass stood against the dramatic rise in violent attacks on blacks by white Americans. In the *Crisis*, W. E. B. Du Bois wrote,

"We return. We return fighting. Make way for Democracy! We saved it and by the Great Jehovah, we will save it in the U. S. A. or know the reason why!" That summer, in twenty-five major cities across the United States, whites rioted in the streets, beating and killing blacks and destroying their property.

This racial violence and hatred was difficult to understand for Pippin and many others who had fought for democracy in the war. It also went against Pippin's upbringing, which stressed the Bible's teachings of brotherhood and harmony. Pippin was also deeply frustrated that he had no outlet for his conflicting memories and emotions of his life as a soldier and his peaceful life in Goshen. At times such as these, he truly felt the loss of his right arm, the one he used to draw.

In the winter of 1925, after having tried and failed to draw with charcoal on the lids of old cigar boxes, Pippin spied the poker resting in the coal-burning kitchen stove. He remembered when growing up in Goshen that there was a popular hobby of drawing by burning designs on wood. It was called pyrography. Pippin quickly set to work with the poker, and it made him feel like his old self again.

Because of the weakness of his right arm, Pippin had to balance his right hand on his crossed legs and draw by moving the wooden board around with his good left hand. It was difficult and tiresome work, as he often had to return the poker to the fire to heat it up again so that he could continue. Also, because he was burning the outlines directly into the wood, he could not make any mistakes since he could not simply erase them. But the daily exercise strengthened his crippled arm, and after a year he became able to lift it and even use it to apply paint to his burnt boards.

In Pippin's burnt wood paintings, home is the strongest theme. Home represented the past for Pippin—his days growing up in Goshen, living in harmony with nature. Pippin had no formal art training, but he produced perfectly balanced scenes of deep emotion and great tranquillity. He once stated, "My opinion of art is that a man should have a love for it because it is my idea that he paints from his heart and his mind. To me it seems impossible to teach one of art."

Pippin found much to record from his memories and from stories his grandmother had told him. He filled his paintings with all the details that he remembered. These paintings captured in a simple, direct way, the solemn dignity of rural black life.

Pippin's paintings were "discovered" by wealthy critic and historian Christian Braton. Through his efforts and those of art patron Albert C. Barnes, Pippin's work received national acclaim and was displayed in New York's Museum of Modern Art. But Pippin was not much impressed with critics, museums, or wealthy collectors. None of those things eased his troubled feelings or provided the peaceful tranquillity that he sought in his paintings. He died in 1946.

Horace Pippin did not rely on previous artists' works for training or inspiration. His art was based wholly on his own life experiences and his vision as an African-American. It was a perfect example of what some in the Harlem Renaissance called for—a fresh conception of black American identity and the richness and warm relationships of black life in America.

Sargent Claude Johnson

Sculptor
1887–1967

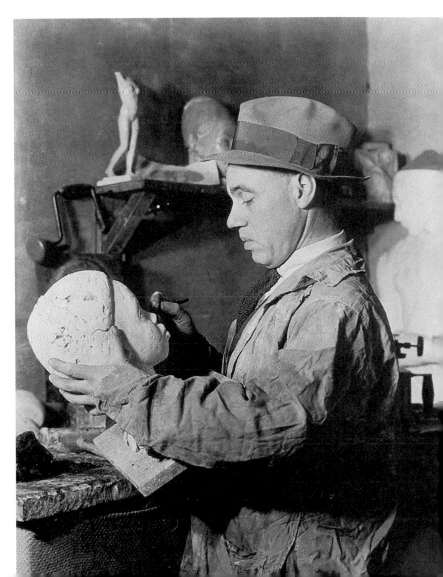

It is the pure American Negro I am concerned with, aiming to show the natural beauty and dignity in that characteristic lip and that characteristic hair, bearing, and manner; and I wish to show that beauty not so much to the white man as to the Negro himself. Unless I can interest my race, I am sunk.

Sargent Claude Johnson, the third of six children, was born in Boston on October 7, 1887. Johnson was of mixed race, and racial identity would be the cornerstone of his art. Sargent's father, Anderson Johnson, was Swedish. His mother, Lizzie Jackson Johnson, was of mixed race—African-American and Cherokee Indian.

Life was very difficult for the Johnsons. Many people did not approve of marriages between blacks and whites and treated them badly. Because of this, Sargent's father had a hard time finding work or decent housing for the family. Anderson Johnson died when Sargent was only ten years old.

Sargent's mother was also very ill so the children were sent to their mother's brother, Sherman William Jackson. His wife was May Howard Jackson and watching her create sculptures had a lasting effect on Sargent. The children were later sent to live with their mother's parents, but raising six children was too hard on the aging couple. In 1902, Sargent's mother died and his brothers and sisters were split up. The girls were sent to a Catholic school for African-American and Native American children in Pennsylvania. The boys were sent to the Sisters of Charity Orphanage in Massachusetts. That was the last time Sargent ever saw his sisters.

Sargent claimed his African-American heritage, but not all of his siblings were comfortable with being black. Some claimed a Native American identity while others passed for white.

Johnson enrolled in a night-school course in drawing and painting and for reasons that are unknown decided that he would go to San Francisco. There, Johnson enrolled in drawing and painting classes at the A. W. Best School of Art.

When he was twenty-eight, Johnson married Pearl Lawson. She was also of mixed ancestry—African-American, English, and French Creole. San Francisco was quite different from the East Coast of America. People of different races and cultures mixed more freely and accepted racial differences more readily. In that welcoming atmosphere, Johnson decided that he would devote himself to becoming a sculptor like his Aunt May. At the time of his decision, he was thirty-two years old.

He enrolled at the California School of Fine Arts and studied under two of the best-known sculptors on the West Coast, Ralph Stackpole and Benjamino Bufano. Sculpture was viewed very differently on the West Coast than it was in the industrial centers of Chicago and New York.

In San Francisco, European ideas of sculpture had little influence. Instead, there were the traditions of Asian art brought by Chinese immigrants, American sailors, and wealthy collectors. There were also the tall, solemn, totem poles from the Native Americans of British Columbia, Canada. In addition, California artists were strongly influenced by the ancient cultures of the Aztec and Maya of Mexico and Central America.

None of these were anything like the neoclassical or realistic sculptures of Europe. Instead, these traditions relied on simple, highly polished surfaces and were often colorfully painted.

Johnson was amazed by the diversity of these cultures and by their deeply spiritual nature. He read Alain Locke's book *The New Negro: An Interpretation* and discussed the ideas in it with other artists. He learned of the touring exhibits of African art from the Congo, and he longed to assert his identity as a black American artist.

Johnson constantly experimented with new techniques and materials such as colored glaze and figures molded in porcelain. Each new experiment brought unexpected delights of form and color. These were wonderful inspirations that kept him going when friends and employers tried to discourage his artistic ambition.

Johnson and his wife, Pearl, were blessed with a baby girl in 1923. They named the child Pearl Adele, and she became Johnson's pride and joy. Because of his daughter, Johnson found himself fascinated with the beauty and innocence of children. He made many portraits of his daughter and other children of the neighborhood. His sculptural portrait of a Chinese neighbor's child, *Elizabeth Gee* (1925), earned Johnson recognition in the newspapers. That same year his portrait of *Pearl* won a medal at the San Francisco Art Exhibition.

Sargent got the attention of the Harmon Foundation and was invited to exhibit his work in 1926. In 1928, he won the Otto H. Kahn prize for *Sammy,* a portrait of a black child. Then, in 1929, he won the Harmon bronze medal and his works were added to the Harmon traveling exhibits that toured the nation. Thousands saw his unique style, and his fame grew.

Some art critics said that his work was fine for decoration but was not "serious" sculpture. They were used to European styles and did not see the merit of Johnson's unique skills. But Johnson did not let them tell him how to sculpt. He just kept on creating new works with his own original vision.

In 1935, Johnson created what some call his greatest sculpture—*Forever Free.* He created the piece by carving and painting wood using techniques from Egypt, Asia, and Africa. Johnson portrayed a black mother with her two children held close to her sides, within her protecting arms. Her face is lifted, looking up and out with hope as she stands firm over her children. *Forever Free* was an instant success.

When the *San Francisco Chronicle* interviewed Johnson about his life and work, he told them:

> *I am producing strictly a Negro art, studying not the culturally mixed Negro of the cities, but the more primitive slave type as existed in this country during the period of slave importation. Very few artists have gone into the history of the Negro in America, cutting back to the sources and origins of the life of the race in this country. . . .*
>
> *I am interested in applying color to sculpture as the Egyptian, Greek and other ancient people did. I try to apply color without destroying the natural expression of sculpture, putting it on pure and in large masses. . . .*

I am concerned with color . . . as a means of heightening the racial character of my work. The Negroes are a colorful race; they call for an art as colorful as they can be made.

Sargent Claude Johnson died of a heart attack in San Francisco on October 10, 1967. He was eighty years old. His intense racial pride and study of non-European sculpture led him to create some of the most unusual Harlem Renaissance art. Proud of his heritage, he showed that simple yet dramatic beauty could be found by blending the art forms of different cultures. His great gift to the Harlem Renaissance was the beauty of harmony in diversity.

Augusta Christine Savage

Sculptor, Activist, and Educator
1892–1962

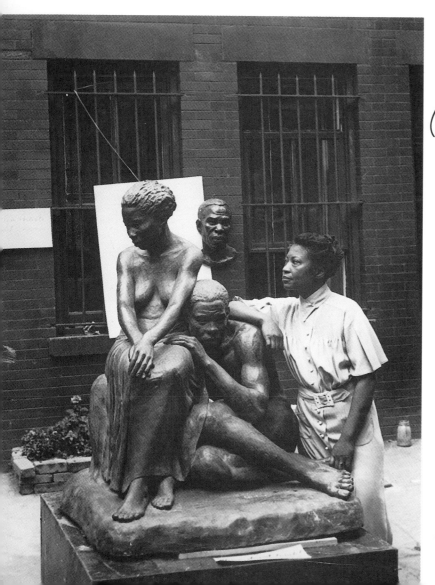

Democracy is a strange thing. My brother was good enough to be accepted in one of the regiments that saw service in France during the war, but it seems his sister is not good enough to be a guest of the country for which he fought. . . . How am I to compete with other American artists if I am not to be given the same opportunity?

It is a sad fact of history that African-Americans have missed out on success, not because of a lack of talent or skills, but because of a lack of opportunity. Augusta Christine Savage's artistic career suffered because she refused to accept racism quietly. Fortunately, she left us a lasting legacy by teaching her skills to a younger generation. They went on to reach the heights that prejudice had denied Augusta.

The seventh of fourteen children, Augusta was born on February 29, 1892, in Cove Springs, Florida. Her father, the Reverend Edward Fells, and her mother, Cornelia, were very poor. They could not afford to buy toys, so Augusta learned to make her own by molding tiny animals with clay.

The soil in Cove Springs was different from the soil in other towns— it was red, sticky clay. Augusta used it to make ducks, chickens, and even playful puppies, but her father did not understand her artistic talent. The Bible said making "graven images" was wrong, so when he caught Augusta making clay animals, he beat her. "My father licked me five or six times a week and almost whipped all the art out of me," she said.

The family moved to West Palm Beach, Florida, when her father was given a ministry there. West Palm Beach did not have red clay like Cove Springs. When she was fifteen years old, however, Augusta spotted the Chase Pottery Factory and begged Mr. Chase for a bucket of clay. Her teacher at Tallahassee State Normal School (now Florida A&M) convinced Reverend Fells to let Augusta keep the clay, and the next day her father regretted all those beatings. She had made a beautiful, 18-inch statue of the Virgin Mary. Her teacher was so impressed that he convinced the school board to pay Augusta $1 a day to teach other students how to mold clay.

Following advice, Savage went to New York for professional training. She arrived with her determination, $4.60, and earned entry into Cooper Union in October 1921. Savage passed the first year's requirements in two weeks. She passed the second year's training in a month. But by February

Gamin, *by Augusta Christine Savage*

1922, she could no longer afford the tuition. However, Savage had so impressed the faculty with her talent that an emergency meeting of the Cooper Union Advisory Council was called. They voted to supply her with tuition, room and board, and even her carfare! It was the first time in the school's history that it had done this for a student.

In 1923, Savage applied for admission to a summer program in Fontainebleau, France, sponsored by the French government. Savage's application was turned down, however, because the selection committee felt that she would be "embarrassed" by having to live and work so closely with the white "southern girls" they had already accepted.

The fact that liberal and educated artists were practicing racial discrimination made front-page news in New York. Ministers and scholars rallied behind Savage's cause. Her response was printed in the May 23 edition of the *New York World:* "This is the first year the school is open and I am the first colored girl to apply. I don't like to see them establish a precedent." Though the committee refused to change its ruling, or answer the negative publicity, clearly they were the ones who were embarrassed.

That incident brought Savage national attention and symbolized the struggle of the New Negro against racism, but it had its price. Savage had criticized some very important people in the art world, and they would neither forget nor forgive her for exposing their prejudice. She was labeled a troublemaker. No one can say how many times she was excluded from galleries and museums because of that dispute.

In 1923, the Harlem branch of the New York Public Library commissioned Savage to create a portrait bust of W. E. B. Du Bois. The critical acclaim of that piece led to more commissions including one of Du Bois's most vocal opponent, Marcus Garvey. She also made many small portraits of the ordinary people of Harlem. One of these became her most famous work—a portrait of a street kid titled *Gamin.* Her portrait captured the boy's cocky attitude and streetwise expression. It immediately became a symbol of all the homeless young people surviving on their wits and courage. Even now, some seventy years later, it is almost impossible to look upon it and not be moved.

Eugene Kinckle Jones of the National Urban League and real estate operator John E. Nail decided that a way must be found for Savage to study in Europe. Jones approached the Rosenwald Fund. Their art critic was so impressed that he awarded not one, but two back-to-back fellowships and increased the amount from $1,500 to $1,800 per year because of Savage's skill and financial needs.

Black Americans everywhere remembered the Fontainebleau incident, and they came forward with donations so that all her award money could go to classes, materials, and living expenses. There were fund-raising parties in Harlem and in Greenwich Village, New York. Black teachers at Florida A&M sent $50. Organizations of black women from various places sent in donations. They were common people who knew what discrimination felt like, and they wanted to help a black woman with the talent to overcome it.

Savage enrolled at the Académie de la Grande Chaumière in Paris in September 1929. In 1930, she won recognition in both the fall and spring Paris Salons, and an African figure she made was reproduced as a medallion at the French Colonial Exposition.

She returned to America in 1931 with renewed confidence, but the Great Depression had brought the sale of artworks to a halt. Savage had no wealthy patron to support her. Even the influential Alain Locke was not interested, possibly because Savage did not agree with his theories on the importance of the "ancestral arts."

Turning her energies away from her own work, Savage concentrated on teaching young black people in New York. She taught anyone who wanted to learn, believing that everyone had some artistic ability. Norman Lewis,

William Artis, Ernest Crichlow, Gwendolyn Bennett, and Jacob Lawrence all benefited greatly from her inspiring instruction.

Augusta Christine Savage died on March 27, 1962. Unfortunately, few of her sculptures have survived. Her legacy, however, can be seen in the work of her students to whom she taught not only artistic technique but also racial pride.

Her school grew to become the Harlem Community Art Center, the largest art center in the United States, and she passed on her gifts freely. Augusta stated, "If I can inspire one of these youngsters to develop the talent I know they possess, then my monument will be their work. No one could ask for more than that."

James Lesesne Wells

Painter and Printmaker
1902–1993

Few artists were able to combine Alain Locke's ideal of looking to Africa for artistic inspiration while creating works that were meaningful to modern African-Americans. James Lesesne Wells's long, successful career extended well into his eighties and included passing on his wealth of knowledge to younger generations of black artists. James was concerned that most blacks could not afford original works of art by their own people, so he took up the art of printmaking. This allowed more African-Americans to own pieces of their rich and growing artistic heritage.

James often used Bible stories, featuring blacks as the subjects of his paintings and prints. But that was only natural because he was the son of a Baptist minister. As a child, James painted stenciled designs along the walls of the prayer-meeting room in his father's church.

James was born on November 2, 1902, in Atlanta, Georgia. His father was Reverend Frederick W. Lesesne Wells, and his mother, Hortensia Ruth Lesesne Wells, was a schoolteacher. His mother, an accomplished artist herself, went on to become the dean of women at Morris Brown University in Atlanta. She encouraged James's artistic ability and gave him crayons and watercolors to experiment with.

Mrs. Wells started a kindergarten after her husband's death, and James became her "teaching assistant." He walked about the room helping children with their drawings and making suggestions for improvements. He was a natural at teaching artistic expression.

Wells had a scholarship to go to the Florida Normal and Industrial Institute. A "normal school" trained people to become teachers, and the Florida Normal and Industrial Institute in Jacksonville, Florida, was designed to prepare young people for teacher's college. During his first year there, thirteen-year-old Wells won first prize in painting and second prize in woodworking at the Florida State Fair.

Wells had earned another scholarship, this one for Lincoln University near Philadelphia, Pennsylvania. But he decided to go to New York first. He wanted to work for the summer so that he would have some savings to go along with his scholarship. He stayed with relatives in Harlem and worked as a porter on the Hudson River Day Line. Financial troubles forced Wells to stay in Harlem for two years. While there, he studied for one term at the National Academy of Design.

Wells finally made it to Lincoln University but only stayed for a year because they did not have an arts program. He transferred to the Teacher's College at Columbia University in New York in 1923. Once there, he was able to combine his two loves, art and teaching, by studying art education.

An exciting event took place in 1923, shortly after Wells returned to New York City. The Brooklyn Museum of Art treated New Yorkers to a rare exhibit, one of New York's first showings of African art. The beauty and simplicity of the African carvings amazed Wells. He came back to the exhibit many times to study those powerful sculptures.

At the same time, in his classes Wells learned about artists from Europe who called themselves expressionists. They felt that what was important in painting and printmaking was expressing the essence of the subject, not copying how things and people appeared in real life. They used bright, unnatural colors and simplified shapes to "express" their feelings about the things they painted. Wells was amazed to learn that they, too, were inspired by African art. In fact, African art was inspiring artists all over Europe to break out of their stuffy, old traditions and create new forms of art.

When Wells graduated from college, he found that magazines such as *Opportunity,* the *Crisis, Survey Graphic,* and others needed artists to illustrate their articles. He created many prints with the methods he learned in school and sold them to the magazines.

James V. Herring, the head of the Howard University Art Department in Washington, D.C., was impressed with Wells's unique and modern maga- azine illustrations. He invited Wells to come to Howard and teach. Wells accepted.

In 1930, Wells won $400 and the gold medal in the annual Harmon Foundation competition. His entry was a painting titled *The Flight into Egypt.* It was based on the biblical story and was very different from the realistic style that most other American painters were using at that time. But what really made Wells's painting so unusual was his use of bright, expressive colors to add energy and impact, and his lack of realistic detail. Many artists become overly dramatic when painting religious scenes, but Wells had a fresh, new approach. Wells won many more prizes in the following years with his modern new style and printmaking techniques.

The stock-market crash of 1929 signaled the beginning of the Great Depression. Year after year, the economy worsened. Many people felt that the cost of original paintings made it impossible for them to own fine works of art. Prints, lithographs, woodcuts, etchings, and serigraphs—methods of making multiple prints of a work of art—were affordable ways for black people to own the beautiful and thought-provoking works of art made by talented African-Americans. Around 1934, Wells decided to devote himself to printmaking. He produced many prints on themes such as black history, manual labor, Bible stories, and Africa.

Much success followed Wells's efforts. He won many competitions, and his prints, etchings, woodcuts, and paintings are now owned by people all over the world. He retired from Howard University in 1968 and continued creating new works of art well into his eighties.

Wells was honored in 1991 with a Living Legend Award for his lifetime of contributions to African-American art and education. He died in Washington, D.C., on January 20, 1993. James Lesesne Wells lives on through his contributions as an educator, artistic innovator, and a leader of the Harlem Renaissance's credo—to combine the inspiration of the ancestral African arts with a modern vision of African-American identity.

More Extraordinary People of the Harlem Renaissance

James Latimer Allen *(1907–1977)*   *Photographer*

A professional photographer who specialized in portraiture. Allen maintained a studio on West 121st Street in Harlem, New York, where he photographed many writers and poets of the New Negro movement. His photographs appeared regularly in the *Crisis* and *Opportunity* magazines.

William Ellisworth Artis *(1914–1977)*   *Sculptor*

Artis studied pottery and sculpture at Augusta Savage's studio. He also worked as an instructor at Harlem's 135th Street branch of the YMCA. Both the Harmon Foundation and the Julius Rosenwald Fund awarded Artis William fellowships. His art appeared in exhibitions sponsored by the Harmon Foundation, the Whitney Museum of Art, the Museum of Modern Art, and many others.

Josephine Baker (*1906–1975*) *Dancer and entertainer*

Baker made her stage debut in the all-black revue *Shuffle Along*. She also danced in the Cotton Club in Harlem. In 1925, Baker moved to Paris where she became a star of stage and film.

Gwendolyn Bennett (*1902–1982*) *Writer*

Artist, poet, and short-story writer, Bennett designed many covers for the *Crisis*. Her column in *Opportunity* magazine, "The Ebony Flute," highlighted the works of the Harlem creative community. "Wedding Day," one of her most acclaimed stories, was featured in the literary magazine *Fire!!*

Leslie Garland Bolling (*1898–1955*) *Sculptor*

Bolling's best-known work was a series of carvings named for every day of the week. His sculpture *Cousin-on Friday* was part of Carl Van Vechten's art collection. Bolling carved figures of local personalities, such as athletes, postmen, potters, and parsons. He exhibited with the Harmon Foundation and other organizations and galleries.

Charles Waddell Chesnutt (*1858–1932*) *Writer*

The first African-American writer to have his work appear in the *Atlantic Monthly* literary magazine, Chesnutt was considered America's first great African-American novelist. His work inspired many writers of the Harlem Renaissance. He was awarded the Spingarn Medal in 1928 by the National Association for the Advancement of Colored People for his pioneering literary efforts, which included such books as *The Conjure Woman* (1899) and *The House behind the Cedars* (1900).

Allan Rohan Crite *(1910– ?)*   *Artist*
Crite's illustrations appeared in the *Crisis, Opportunity, Survey Graphic,* the *Boston Globe,* and Charles Woodbury's *The Art of Seeing* (1925). He is best known for his portraits and street scenes. Crite's later work focused on religious art. His black-and-white drawings were published in a series of illustrated books that included *Were You There When They Crucified My Lord?* (1944) and *All Glory* (1947).

Charles Clarence Dawson *(1889–1981)*   *Painter*
Dawson dedicated his art to portrayals of everyday black life. He founded the Chicago Art League, a club for black artists which met at the Wabash Avenue YMCA during the 1920s. Dawson was a staff artist for a newspaper, a muralist, and a freelance painter and illustrator. In 1933, he published *ABC of Great Negroes,* which featured his drawings of twenty-six black leaders.

Beauford Delaney *(1902–1977)*   *Painter*
Delany painted a number of African-American writers, musicians, and intellectuals. His pastel and oil portraits were featured in a one-man exhibit at the Harlem library in 1930. In 1953, Delaney moved to Paris.

James Reese Europe *(1881–1919)*   *Composer, conductor, and bandleader*
Known for his popular Clef Club, Europe's success as an African-American entertainer opened the door to other black performers such as Eubie Blake and Noble Sissle. His orchestras specialized in music by black composers. Europe helped Blake and Sissle produce their vaudeville shows. The three had planned to join forces in music after World War I, but Europe's career was cut short when he was stabbed by a fellow bandmember.

William McKnight Farrow *(1885–1967)*   *Artist and writer*

Farrow was an exhibit designer and lecturer at the Chicago Art Institute. In the 1920s, he started a Christmas-card business. His art was featured in exhibitions in Chicago, New York, and throughout the United States. The American Art Dealers Association selected his lithograph *Peace* as one of the fifty best American prints in 1933. His column "Art in the Home" was a regular feature in the *Chicago Defender*. Through his writing, he also documented the activity of Chicago's arts community.

Julian Fauntleroy   *Harlem celebrity*

Fauntleroy was a man from Trinidad who enlisted and trained with the Royal Canadian Air Corps during World War I. In Harlem, he became an officer in Garvey's UNIA and a community celebrity.

Arthur Huff Fauset *(1889–1983)*   *Writer*

An anthropologist and folklorist dedicated to preserving the folklore and black folk culture of the South, Fauset was among the artists and writers who contributed to Wallace Thurman's magazine, *Fire!!* His essays appeared in *Opportunity* magazine. Fauset also wrote for the NAACP's children's publication, the *Brownies Book*. He was the half-brother of the *Crisis* editor Jessie Fauset.

Rudolph Fisher *(1897–1934)*   *Writer*

A doctor and a writer, Fisher ran an X-ray laboratory in Harlem and was the superintendent of Harlem's International Hospital. Though he died young, he was considered one of the best writers of the Harlem Renaissance. His best-known books are *The Walls of Jericho* and *The Conjure-Man Dies,* which is thought to be the first black detective novel published in book form.

Rabbis Arnold Ford and Wentworth Hubert *Religious leaders*

Ford and Hubert founded the Black Jews of Harlem—one of the oldest and largest Hebrew-Israelite groups in the United States. They established Beth B'nai Abraham Congregation at 29 West 131st Street.

Randall Freelon *(1895–1960)* *Artist and editor*

A member of the Philadelphia group of artists and writers associated with the New Negro movement, Freelon was editor of the short-lived literary magazine *Black Opals* (1927–1928). His art was featured in Harlem exhibitions in the 1920s and 1930s. In 1935, he participated in a controversial art show, Commentary on Lynching.

Angelina Weld Grimké *(1880–1958)* *Poet and Writer*

Though Grimké did not reside in Harlem, her poetry, prose, and short-stories were an important feature of the Harlem Renaissance. Grimké work was performed at the Harlem YMCA by the W. E. B. Du Bois Krigwa Players.

John Wesley Hardwick *(1891–1968)* *Painter*

Hardwick won the Harmon Foundation bronze medal in fine arts in 1927. He also painted several murals on churches and schools in Indianapolis, his birthplace.

Edwin Augustus Harleston *(1882–1931)* *Painter*

During the Harlem Renaissance, Harleston was known for his portraits of African-Americans. He and his wife opened a studio that showcased portraits done in oil, charcoal, and photography. He was awarded the NAACP Spingarn Award from the *Crisis* for his painting *Ouida*, a painting of his wife. Harleston assisted Aaron Douglas with his famous murals for the library at Fisk University.

William Angier Jennings *(1910–)*   *Painter and printmaker*
Jennings's art was greatly influenced by Hale Woodruff. He was employed by the Works Progress Administration (WPA) in the graphics department. He also designed stage sets and jewelry.

Eva Jessye *(1895–1992)*   *Choir director*
Jessye's choir toured throughout the United States. She also helped to train numerous black choruses and promoted the performance of black spirituals.

Malvin Gray Johnson *(1896–1934)*   *Painter*
Johnson was known for his paintings of Harlem street scenes and for works inspired by Negro spirituals. His work *Swing Low, Sweet Chariot* won "best painting" in the 1929 Harmon Foundation exhibition.

Ferdinand Joseph LaMenthe (Jelly Roll Morton) *(1885–1941)*   *Musician*
Jazz pianist and pioneer organizer of the large jazz orchestra, Morton's group, the Red Hot Chili Peppers, blended blues, ragtime, jazz, Creole, and Spanish sounds.

"Pig Foot Mary"   *Popular Harlem success story*
 Pig Foot Mary walked the streets of Harlem daily pushing a baby carriage from which she sold chitterlings, corn, hogmaw, and pigs' feet. She even invented a portable steam table to warm the food she sold. Mary saved her money and invested more than $375,000 in Harlem real estate.

Rose McClendon *(1885–1936)*   *Actress*

McClendon was the star of the stage version of the Pulitzer Prize–winning novel *Abraham's Bosom,* among other roles. Paul Robeson called her "the leading actress of the Negro race." McClendon was also referred to as the Dark Duse and the Sepia Barrymore.

Florence Mills *(1895–1927)*   *Actress*

One of the most loved entertainers of the 1920s, Mills made her stage debut in *Shuffle Along.* Mills became the first black female star to win international acclaim. She was widely admired by the African-American community for turning down a high-profile role in the Ziegfeld Follies to participate in an all-black revue. When she died in 1927, her funeral was the largest in Harlem's history. More than 5,000 mourners attended and more than 150,000 people crowded the streets in tribute.

Ann Lane Petry *(1909–1997)*   *Writer*

Petry was the first African-American woman to have a best-seller. Her novel *The Street* sold 1.5 million copies and described the life of post-Renaissance Harlem and the despair caused by the Great Depression. She also wrote *Tituba of Salem Village* for young readers and two other novels—*The Country Place* (1947) and *The Narrows* (1953).

Edgar Eugene Phillips *(1887– ?)*   *Photographer*

Phillips was from Jamaica. In the 1920s, he moved to Harlem, New York, and opened his own studio. He photographed the people and nightlife of Harlem.

Robert Savon Pious *(1908–1983)*   *Painter*

In 1931, Pious's portrait of singer Roland Hayes won a Harmon Foundation prize. He also worked as a commercial artist, creating cartoons and book illustrations.

James A. Porter (1903–1970) — *Painter*

Porter was a painter who traveled the world to expose himself to different forms of art. His painting *Woman Holding a Jug* won first prize in the Arthur A. Schomburg Portrait Contest. Porter wrote *Modern Negro Art,* considered one of the most important books ever written on the subject. He also wrote many articles on art.

Gertrude "Ma" Rainey (1886–1939) — *Singer*

Rainey was a blues, jazz, and vaudeville singer. She is one of the most important women in blues history. Her work influenced other singers such as Bessie Smith and Ethel Waters.

Arthur Schomburg (1874–1938) — *Activist, archivist, curator*

Schomburg was a lecturer for the United Negro Improvement Association. In 1922, he headed the American Negro Academy, an organization designed to promote black art, literature, and science. Schomburg curated art exhibits during the Harlem Renaissance at the 135th Street branch of the New York Public Library. He collected thousands of works on black culture over his lifetime. In 1926, Schomburg's personal collection was donated to the New York Public Library and became known as the Schomburg Collection of Negro Literature and History. The name was later changed to the Schomburg Center for Research in Black Culture.

William Edouard Scott (1884–1964) — *Painter*

Scott studied in Paris under Henry Ossawa Tanner, among other artists. His paintings of rural scenes appeared on the covers of the *Crisis.* Many of Scott's pieces were commissioned by W. E. B. Du Bois and displayed in the *Crisis* office.

Morgan and Marvin Smith *(1910–   )*   *Photographers*
These twin brothers documented life in Harlem from the 1930s to the 1950s. A showing of their work *Harlem: The Vision of Morgan and Marvin Smith* was featured at the Schomburg Center for Research in Black Culture. Morgan died in 1993. Marvin still lives in Harlem.

Anne Spencer *(1882–1970)*   *Poet*
Spencer was a poet who used images from her garden and everyday life to make powerful statements about the human condition and race. Her most famous poems are "White Things" and "Lady, Lady." Forty-two of the fifty poems of Anne Spencer can be found in J. Lee Greene's *Time's Unfading Garden: Anne Spencer's Life and Poetry* (1977).

A'Lelia Walker   *Socialite*
Walker was the daughter of the first woman in America to earn $1 million through her own hard work, Madam C. J. Walker. She inherited her mother's wealth and property and was a Harlem socialite. Famous for her tearoom, the Dark Tower, Walker hosted high-society parties frequented by Harlem intellectuals, the international jet set, and even royalty.

Thomas "Fats" Waller *(1904–1943)*   *Jazz Pianist*
A student of jazz pioneer James P. Johnson, Waller wrote the musical score for the Broadway hit *Hot Chocolates,* which featured his most famous song, "Ain't Misbehavin'." Waller is credited with creating the boogie-woogie style of piano jazz.

Eric Walrond *(1898–1966)*   *Writer*
Walrond's stories appeared in *Opportunity* and the *Crisis* magazines. His essays appeared in the *Messenger,* the *New Republic,* and other periodicals. Walrond

was part of the core group that created *Fire!!* His most acclaimed work, *Tropic Death* (1926), was praised by W. E. B. Du Bois and Langston Hughes. *Tropic Death* is a collection of ten stories about inhumanity in the American tropics.

Dorothy West *(1907–1999)*   *Writer*

West tied for first prize with Zora Neale Hurston in *Opportunity* magazine's 1926 literary contest. The youngest of the Harlem literati, she was nicknamed "the Kid." Her first novel, *The Living Is Easy,* was published in 1948. Her most popular novel, *The Wedding,* was published in 1995, when Dorothy was eighty-eight years old.

Walter White *(1893–1955)*   *Activist and writer*

White worked alongside James Weldon Johnson as assistant secretary of the NAACP. He later became executive secretary when Johnson resigned from that post. White wrote the novel *Fire in the Flint* (1924) and an autobiography, *A Man Called White* (1948).

Glossary

abolitionists—people who worked with the Underground Railroad and other groups to end slavery

abstract art—art that represents the artist's feelings about a subject rather than the form of the subject itself. In abstract art, the artist does not try to "copy" the way things look in reality. Instead, the artist uses colors and/or shapes that may look nothing like the subject

anthology—a collection of essays or stories by various writers.

arranger—a person who prepares and writes the musical parts for the instruments and/or vocals of a song

black (or African) nationalism—the belief that black people should be economically independent, self-governing, and in complete control of their own destiny

blackface—a form of entertainment in which white and black performers covered their faces with charred cork and painted on oversized white lips to poke fun at African-Americans. Blackface was used in minstrel shows and in vaudeville.

brothel—a house of prostitution

buck dancer—a folk style of dancing that originated in Africa. It is the basis for the popular jazz dance called the Charleston and for tap dance.

bust—a sculpture of a person's head, shoulders, and chest

cast, casting—the practice of creating a sculpture by first making a mold and then filling it with a liquid such as plaster or molten metal that hardens in the shape of the mold

color line, the—the imaginary boundary that separates black and white people. Used as a figure of speech.

communism—a political system in which the government owns all of the land and businesses, and the profits are supposed to be shared as needed by the people

critic—a person who judges the value and meaning of works of music, art, or literature. For example, art critic, literary critic, or music critic.

dialect—the variety of a language spoken by people of a particular region

expressionism—a movement in the arts during the early twentieth century that encouraged artists to express their unique personal thoughts and experiences. It often involved exaggerating the way things really looked.

fascism—a system of government in which one person (a dictator) has complete power

fellowship—a financial award given to a graduate student in a college or university

folklore—the original culture, myths, tales, and practices of a people

Garveyism—the ideas and concepts of Marcus Garvey, who was a black nationalist. Garveyism was the basis of the Black Power movement of the 1970s.

genre—grouping or category. For example, jazz and blues are two different genres of music.

ghostwriter—a person employed to write a book under the name of another writer

grant—the award of funds for a special purpose

humanism—a concern for the interests, needs, and welfare of human beings

Jim Crow—practices set up to oppress and discriminate against black people

literati—a term used to refer to writers, poets, and other people interested in the arts

milliner—a person who makes or sells hats

modernism—a variety of art forms based on a belief that humankind could reach a state of perfection through evolution, technology, and the use of logical thought. According to modernism, all cultural differences would eventually disappear.

mulatto—a person with one white parent and one black parent

murals—large-scale paintings, usually done on a oversized canvas or walls. Murals are often painted on the sides of buildings for public display.

neoclassical—refers to a style of art that imitates ancient Greek and Roman art

niggerati—a term that came to be used in fun to describe the community of African-American artists, writers, and intellectuals. The word originated from Wallace Thurman's novel *The Infants of Spring* in which the main character resides at "Niggerati Manor."

The Paris Salon—A show in which the the artists and instructors of the French Academy judge and exhibit what they feel is the best art the world has to offer for that year.

passing—pretending to be white; historically done by fair-skinned blacks or mulattoes to avoid the struggles of racism.

patron—someone who provides support.

Phi Beta Kappa—an honor society for college students who have earned exceptional grades

piano roll—a roll of paper used in a player piano to control the movement and sound of the keys

pianola—a mechanically operated piano that plays preprogrammed music from a piano roll

plagiarism—presenting someone else's written work as your own. Plagiarism is unethical and illegal.

primitive—an artist or artwork that appears uneducated, untrained, or lacking in accepted European standards of fine art. Literature written in authentic dialect and folk stories were also considered primitive.

prolific—producing a large number of works

Pullman porter—a railroad employee who assisted passengers with their luggage

Reconstruction era—the period after the Civil War, from 1865 to 1867, when the Confederate states were under the direct control of the federal government before being readmitted to the Union. It was a source of great anger and humiliation for southern whites.

romanticism—a type of art that used vivid color and dramatic scenes to emphasize emotions and high moral standards

scat singing—a style of jazz vocals in which random sounds are sung to the melody

segregation—a separation of the races. For example, separate schools for white children and black children. Segregation usually meant separate and low-quality resources for African-Americans.

socialism—a system or society in which everything is owned and shared by all

sonnet—a fourteen-line poem with a rhyming pattern

statuary—the plural form of statue

stereotype—to apply a particular quality to an entire group of people. Stereotypes usually portray an entire group of people in a negative light.

tercentennial—300-year anniversary

Underground Railroad—a series of secret safe houses and trails used to help slaves escape to freedom in the northern United States and Canada

valedictorian—a student with the highest academic standing in a high school or college graduating class

vaudeville—groups of entertainers who toured the country performing comedy, musical, and dance acts

For Further Information

Books for Younger Readers

ABOUT THE HARLEM RENAISSANCE

Calvert, Roz. *Zora Neale Hurston.* New York: Chelsea House, 1993.

Chambers, Veronica, and B. Mavis. *The Harlem Renaissance.* New York: Chelsea House, 1997.

Ehrlich, Scott, and Steven Samuels (photographer). *Paul Robeson: Singer and Actor.* New York: Chelsea House, 1987.

Everett, Gwen. *Li'L Sis and Uncle Willie: A Story Based on the Life and Paintings of William H. Johnson.* New York: Hyperion Press, 1994.

Hacker, Carlotta. *Great African-Americans in Jazz.* New York: Crabtree Publishing, 1997.

Kallen, Stuart A., *The Twentieth Century and the Harlem Renaissance: A History of Black People in America, 1880–1930.* Minneapolis: Abdo & Daughters, 1990.

Levine, Gail Carson. *Dave at Night.* New York: HarperCollins Children's Books, 1999.

Lewis, Zoe. *Keisha Discovers Harlem.* New York: Magic Attic, 1998.

McDaniel, Melissa. *W. E. B. Du Bois: Scholar and Civil Rights Activist.* Danbury, Conn.: Franklin Watts, 1999.

McKissack, Patricia, and Frederick McKissack. *Zora Neale Hurston: Writer and Storyteller.* Springfield, N.J.: Enslow Publishers, 1992.

Medearis, Angela Shelf. *Little Louis and the Jazz Band: The Story of Louis "Satchmo" Armstrong.* New York: Dutton, 1994.

Monceaux, Morgan, and Wynton Marsalis. *Jazz: My Music, My People.* New York: A.A. Knopf, 1994.

Orgill, Roxanne. *If I Only Had a Horn: Young Louis Armstrong.* Boston: Houghton Mifflin, 1997.

Osofsky, Audrey. *Free to Dream: The Making of a Poet, Langston Hughes.* New York: Lothrop Lee & Shepard, 1996.

Pinkney, Andrea Davis. *Duke Ellington: The Piano Prince and His Orchestra.* New York: Disney Press, 1998.

Schroeder, Allan. *Ragtime Tumpie.* Boston: Little Brown & Company, 1989.

———. *Satchmo's Blues.* New York: Doubleday, 1996.

Silverman, Jerry (ed.). *Ragtime Song and Dance* (Traditional Black Music). Chelsea House, 1995.

Venezia, Mike, *Duke Ellington.* Chicago: Childrens Press, 1995.

Vigna, Guiseppe. *Jazz and Its History.* New York: Barrons Juveniles, 1999.

By Writers of the Harlem Renaissance

Bontemps, Arna, and Langston Hughes. *The Pasteboard Bandit.* New York: Oxford University Press, 1997.

Bontemps, Arna, and Langston Hughes; edited by E. Simms Campbell. *Popo and Fifina.* New York: Oxford University Press, 1993.

Cullen, Countee, J. *The Lost Zoo.* Englewood Cliffs, N.J.: Silver Burdett Press, 1991.

Giovanni, Nikki (ed.). *Shimmy Shimmy Shimmy Like My Sister Kate: Looking at the Harlem Renaissance Through Poems.* New York: Henry Holt, 1996.

Hughes, Langston. *Black Misery.* New York: Oxford University Press, 1994.

_____ . *The Book of Rhythms.* New York: Oxford University Press, 1995.

Johnson-Feelings, Dianne (ed.) *The Best of the Brownies' Book.* New York: Oxford University Press, 1996.

Johnson, James Weldon. *The Creation.* New York: Holiday House, 1995.

_____ . *Lift Every Voice and Sing.* New York: Walker & Co., 1993.

Books for Older Readers

ABOUT THE HARLEM RENAISSANCE

Candaele, Kerry, Spencer Crew, Clayborne Carson (ed.), and Darlene Clark Hine (ed). *Bound for Glory 1910–1930: From the Great Migration to the Harlem Renaissance.* New York: Chelsea House, 1996.

Gayle, Addison Jr. *The Black Aesthetic.* New York: Anchor Books, 1972.

Harris, Trudier. *Afro-American Writers from the Harlem Renaissance to 1940.* Dictionary of Literary Biography. Volume 51. Detroit: Gale, 1986.

Huggins, Nathan Irvin. *Harlem Renaissance.* New York: Oxford University Press, 1971.

Jacques, Geoffrey. *Free within Ourselves: The Harlem Renaissance.* Danbury, Conn.: Franklin Watts, 1996.

Jakoubek, Robert E. *Walter White and the Power of Organized Protest.* Brookfield, Conn.: Millbrook Press, 1994.

Jones, Hettie. *Big Star Fallin Mama: Five Women in Black Music.* New York: Puffin Books, 1997.

Kimball, Robert, and William Bolcom. *Reminiscing with Sissle and Blake.* New York: Viking Press, 1973.

Lawler, Mary, and Nathan I. Huggins (ed.). *Marcus Garvey: Black Nationalist Leader.* New York: Chelsea House, 1987.

Reynolds, Gary A., and Beryl J. Wright. *Against the Odds: African-American Artists and the Harmon Foundation*. Newark, N.J.: The Newark Museum, 1989.

Roses, Lorraine E. *Harlem Renaissance and Beyond: Literary Biographies of 100 Black Women Writers, 1900–1945*. Boston: G. K. Hall, 1990.

Sundquist, Eric J. *The Hammers of Creation: Folk Culture in Modern African-American Fiction*. Athens, Ga.: University of Georgia Press, 1992.

Tyler, Bruce Michael. *From Harlem to Hollywood: The Struggle for Racial and Cultural Democracy, 1920–1943*. New York: Garland Publishing, 1992.

Vincent, Theodore (ed.). *Voices of a Black Nation: Political Journalism in the Harlem Renaissance*. San Francisco: Ramparts Press, 1973.

BY WRITERS OF THE HARLEM RENAISSANCE

Bontemps, Arna, *Black Thunder; Gabriel's Revolt: Virginia 1800*. 1936. Boston: Beacon, paper, 1992.

Cullen, Countee, *Color*. New York: Arno Press, 1969.

Du Bois, W. E. B. *The Souls of Black Folk*. New York: The New American Library, 1982.

Fauset, Jessie Redmon. *The Chinaberry Tree: A Novel of American Life*. 1931. Reprint with an introduction by Thadious Davis. Boston: G. K. Hall, 1995.

———. *Comedy: American Style* (1933). Reprint with an introduction by Thadious M. Davis. Boston: G. K. Hall, 1995.

_____ . *Plum Bun: A Novel without a Moral.* 1929. Reprint with a new introduction by Deborah E. McDowell. Boston: Pandora Press, 1985.

_____ . *There Is Confusion.* 1924. Reprint with a new foreword by Thadious M. Davis. Boston: Northeastern University Press, 1989.

Handy, W. C., and Arna Bontemps (ed). *Father of the Blues: An Autobiography.* New York: Da Capo Press, 1991.

Harper, Michael S. (ed.). *The Collected Poems of Sterling A. Brown.* New York: Harper & Row, 1980.

Hurston, Zora Neale. *The Complete Stories.* New York: HarperPerennial Library, 1996.

Hurston, Zora Neale, and Alice Walker (ed). *I Love Myself When I Am Laughing. . . and Then Again When I Am Looking Mean and Impressive: A Zora Neale Hurston Reader.* Old Westbury, N. Y. : Feminist Press, 1989.

Hurston, Zora Neale, and Pamela Bordelon (ed.). *Go Gator and Muddy the Water: Writings by Zora Neale Hurston from the Federal Writers Project.* New York: W. W. Norton, 1999.

McKay, Claude, and Wayne M. Cooper. *Home to Harlem.* Boston: Northeastern University Press, 1987.

Thurman, Wallace. *The Blacker the Berry . . . .* 1929. Reprinted with a new introduction by Shirlee Taylor Haizlip. New York: Simon and Schuster, 1996.

_____ . *Infants of Spring.* New York: Modern Library, 1999.

Waldo, Terry, and Eubie Blake. *This Is Ragtime.* New York: De Capo Press, 1991.

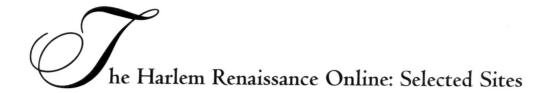

The Harlem Renaissance Online: Selected Sites

The Academy of American Poets—Poetry Exhibits—Harlem Renaissance
http://www.poets.org/lit/exh/EX006.htm

Arna Bontemps African-American Museum and Cultural Arts Center
http://www.lacollege.edu/~bontemps/Arnabontempsmain.html

Arna Bontemps Poetry
http://www.sas.upenn.edu/~vbead/Bontemps.html

W. E. B. Du Bois Virtual University
http://members.tripod.com/~DuBois/index.html

Harlem 1900–1940: An African-American Community
http://www.si.umich.edu/CHICO/Harlem/
An online exhibit from the Schomburg Center for Research in Black Culture.

Harlem Renaissance
http://www.lincolnu.edu/~kluebber/harlit.htm
This site explores the Harlem Renaissance—complete with definitions and color photos.

Harlem Renaissance

Explores the poetry, politics, women, jazz, and theater of the Harlem Renaissance.

http://www.geocities.com/Athens/Forum/4722/big.html

Harlem Renaissance

http://www.iniva.org/harlem/chron.html

A brief chronology.

Harlem Renaissance: An Introduction

http://www.csustan.edu/english/reuben/pal/chap9/9intro.html

Overview and examination of the Harlem Renaissance, along with information on the writers and literary works of that era.

The Harlem Renaissance

http://www.unc.edu/courses/eng81br1/harlem.html

The Harlem Renaissance and Black Popular Culture

http://www.middlebury.edu/~ac400/Group_3/template3.html

Shows many of the significant figures who contributed to the cultural movement known as the Harlem Renaissance.

Langston Hughes Links

http://www.liben.com/Hugheslinks.html

Langston Hughes and the Harlem Renaissance

http://www.si.edu/tsa/disctheater/sweet/tss03.htm

Painters of the Harlem Renaissance

http://www.nku.edu/~diesmanj/PAINTERS.HTML

Showcases a collection of paintings by Harlem Renaissance artists.

Poetry of the Harlem Renaissance

http://www.poetsworld.com/harlem.htm

The Poetry of Langston Hughes

http://www.novia.net/~aaronk/ls/hughes.html

Poetry and Prose of the Harlem Renaissance

http://www.nku.edu/~Harlem/diesmanj/poetryindex.htm

Rhapsodies in Black: Art of the Harlem Renaissance

http://www.tfaoi.com/newsmu/nmus5e.htm

The Signifying Monkey: Webliography of the Pan African Diaspora

http://www.csun.edu/~hcpas003/

Extensive site on African-American history. Includes special section on the Harlem Renaissance.

Women of the Harlem Renaissance

http://www.geocities.com/Athens/Forum/4722/harlem2.html

Selected biographies

Music of the Harlem Renaissance Online

http://www.lincolnu.edu/~kluebber/harmus.htm

Harlem Renaissance music links

The Music of Louis Armstrong

http://www.Satchmo.com
and
http://www.capecodonline.com/primetime/armstrong.htm

Jazz

http://www.movingmusic.co.uk/musiccatjazz.htm
A selection of jazz.

Blues

http://www.bluestown.com
A selection of blues music.

Index

Numbers in *italics* represent illustrations.

Photo Credits

Photographs ©: AP/Wide World Photos: cover top far left, cover bottom far right, 7, 9, 53, 125; Archive Photos: back cover top left, 8, 70 (Frank Driggs Collection), 25; Archives of American Art, Smithsonian Institution: 9, 168 (Henry O. Tanner Papers/Photographs of Artists, Collection I); Art Resource, NY: 205 (National Museum of American Art, Washington, D. C.); Brown Brothers: cover top center, cover bottom right, cover bottom left, back cover top center, 3, 7, 8, 9, 19, 57, 66, 74, 77, 79, 99, 131, 146, 171; Chester County Historical Society, Westchester, PA: 10, 230; Corbis-Bettmann: cover top right, cover bottom far left, back cover top right, 7, 8, 9, 10, 21, 85, 97, 119, 122, 208 (UPI), 7, 8, 17, 38, 94, 103; Danforth Museum of Art Collection: 10, 178; Donna Mussenden Van Der Zee: back cover bottom right, 10, 192 (James Van Der Zee); Fogg Art Museum, Harvard University Art Museums,: 9, 161 (Bequest of Evert Jansen Wendell/Rick Stafford); Frank Driggs Collection: cover top far right, back cover bottom left, 7, 8, 45, 49, 55, 59, 61, 64, 68, 89; Hampton University Museum, Hampton, VA: 153; Howard University Gallery of Art, Washington D. C.: 166; Liaison Agency, Inc.: cover top left, 7, 8, 27, 46, 83, 92 (Hulton Getty); Moorland Spingarn Research Center, Howard University: 9, 10, 143, 174 (Mary O' H. Williamson Collection), 9, 128; National Archives at College Park: 10, 11, 196, 213, 220, 225, 235; National Museum of American Art, Smithsonian Institution: 10, 200; Rhode Island College, Providence, Rhode Island: 10, 182 (Nancy Elizabeth Prophet Collection); Schomburg Center for Research in Black Culture, Art & Artifacts Division, New York Public Library: 242 (Astor, Lenox and Tilden Foundations, Gamin, 1929, Plaster, 9 1/4 x 6 x 3 1/2 D, Gift of Lorraine Lucas), 11, 240 (Herman/Federal Art Project W. P. A.), 10, 186 (Townsend), 8, 9, 11, 29, 111, 139, 155, 246; Whitney Museum of American Art: 217 (Geoffrey Clements Photography); Yale Collection of American Literature, Beinecke Rare Book and Manuscript Library: 7, 8, 9, 33, 107, 115, 135.

About the Authors

*P*Stephen Hardy and Sheila Jackson Hardy collaborate in their work as writers and fine art dealers. Their first writing collaboration was a children's story on Augusta Savage. Stephen is a writer, art historian, and a self-taught artist. His paintings have been featured in galleries across the United States.

Sheila is a freelance writer who enjoys writing children's stories and adult nonfiction. She has written for publications such as *Essence* magazine and is a columnist for the *Sunday Sun* in Barbados, West Indies.